Praise for *Collect*

"Do you ever wonder if you're missing out on your life's calling? Or think you don't have the strength to pursue your dreams? Kim's colorful journey collecting confidence is full of twists and turns, and she invites us along to experience the lessons she's learned and the trust she's found in the only One who can make the most of any messy story."

—Candace Cameron Bure, actress, producer, entrepreneur, *New York Times* bestselling author

"Like Kim herself this book is filled with honesty, home-spun wisdom, and laughs. You will be entertained while getting practical insights to building confidence."

—Rob Sharenow, president of programming, A+E Networks

"With her faith, her ability to see the best when the worst is on display, her love and commitment to life itself, my sister Kim is a national treasure who consistently impacts lives. I'm so proud that her confidence and heart for others leaps off the pages of this masterpiece. Let's go, baby!"

—Deion "Coach Prime" Sanders, Pro Football Hall of Famer; two-time Super Bowl champion; eight-time Pro Bowler; head football coach, University of Colorado Buffaloes

"Kim Gravel is inspiring, genuine, and relatable. *Collecting Confidence* is filled with stories and advice that resonated with me deeply. I respect Kim's willingness to be vulnerable. Her eloquent, humorous, and self-effacing writing style has a wonderful way of bringing in readers and making them feel seen."

—Idina Menzel, Tony Award–winning performer, actress, singer-songwriter, philanthropist, and designer of Encore by Idina

"Kim Gravel does life right. Every time I talk to her, she reminds me of where I'm from and where I'm going. And now, everyone can have access to her wisdom. This book delivers all the charm, beauty, and wisdom of Kim, one page at a time."

—Lance Bass, multi-platinum artist, entrepreneur, TV host

"Kim Gravel is my soul sister. It doesn't matter who you are or where you come from, the stories Kim tells in *Collecting Confidence* are relatable and will change the way you think and feel about yourself. This book is full of love, laughs, and energy. Kim understands that women want confidence, and that's what she delivers in this book."

—Alina Villasante, founder, creator, and visionary, Peace Love World

Collecting
Confidence

Collecting *Confidence*

Start Where You Are to Become the Person You Were Meant to Be

Kim Gravel

An Imprint of Thomas Nelson

Collecting Confidence

Published in Nashville, Tennessee, by Nelson Books, an imprint of Thomas Nelson. Nelson Books and Thomas Nelson are registered trademarks of HarperCollins Christian Publishing, Inc.

The author is represented by Claudia Riemer Boutote, Red Raven Studio.

Thomas Nelson titles may be purchased in bulk for educational, business, fundraising, or sales promotional use. For information, please e-mail SpecialMarkets@ThomasNelson.com.

ISBN 978-1-4002-3860-6 (TP)
ISBN 978-1-4041-1951-2 (CU)
ISBN 978-1-4002-3859-0 (audiobook)
ISBN 978-1-4002-3853-8 (eBook)
ISBN 978-1-4002-3845-3 (HC)

Library of Congress Control Number: 2022952431

Printed in the United States of America

24 25 26 27 28 LBC 5 4 3 2 1

Parenting is not so much what you say or do but who you are. This book is in honor of my mom and dad, Jo and Brooks Hardee, the two people in my life who modeled common sense and uncommon faith, and who walked boldly in their confidence. I love you.

Contents

Why I Wrote This Book

> *You can't go back and change the beginning, but you can start where you are and change the ending.*
>
> —Unknown

Life has a way of knocking the breath out of you.

Sometimes, after one too many punches in the gut, we look for answers—on television, through spiritual practices, and in self-help books. I've personally read more self-help books than Starbucks has drink combinations. And I have thirty-one unused planners and journals to prove it! (I also have more Sharpies than Office Max.)

That's why I wrote this book. I'm looking for answers, and I bet you are too. If you want to know how to repair your marriage, lose thirty pounds, or be a better mom, then you're reading the wrong book. Let me state for the record, this is *not* a self-help book. It could be a self-appreciation book, a self-reflection book, or a self-confidence book but *not,* I repeat, a self-help book. I'm not asking you to help yourself, get healthier, or change at all.

You don't have to *do* anything.

You're not holding a book; you're holding a mirror. Not one of those scary 50x magnifying mirrors that make you think, *When did I turn into Chewbacca*? This is a mirror that will help you see the magnificent, self-assured, beautiful creation you've always been. You might not see her immediately . . . but you'll see her slowly drop her guard, and the true you will emerge.

She's a beauty.

There's nothing new under the sun—except you. Your unique hair (even if it's falling out and gray), your personality (even if you come on too strong or are too shy and submissive), and your skin (whether you're brown like coffee or as white as the creamer). This applies to you whether you are big and curvy or so skinny you can stand under a clothesline in a rainstorm and stay dry.

This book is not about how you categorize yourself or what you've done. Girl, I don't care what you've done. I've done bad things and made horrible decisions, and I'm still here. This is about something much bigger than the mess you may have made of parts of your life. Where you are is where you were meant to be. For now. But there's more for you in your future—good things, beautiful things.

This book will give you permission to be everything you were created to be, starting from right where you are. The truth is that every woman from every walk of life can be exactly who she was meant to be.

Spoiler alert: you were meant to be a person of confidence or, to put it more memorably, a person of tenacity and audacity.

Yes, little ole you. Hard to believe? I'll show you. We're going to have fun! We're going to laugh, cry, and create together. You're gonna pop out of bed with a newfound sense of purpose. Everything you want and long for is possible. I'm a designer, and the most enjoyable part of fashion, to me, is the design process. I get to let my creative juices run wild! *What are we going to make? What's it going to look like? Let's try it this way! Let's try another color!* Imagine how fun it is to start designing your life! Be creative. Life is supposed to be fun, and it's gonna be.

You're not broken. You don't need fixing. But that's a hard pill for some of us to swallow. I want to arm you with ways to protect your heart, mind, and calling, because there are those who want to see you defeated. I want this book to empower you, to help you understand the way you think about yourself, how you see yourself, and the way you talk to yourself.

You're not broken. You don't need fixing.

I want you to truly believe in your own beauty. You are fearfully and wonderfully made; there is no one else like you. Your story and life experiences are unique and useful. You don't have to clean up your act or change a lick to move into the wide-open spacious life you long for deep within.

Sometimes in life our confidence waxes or wanes, but the most important thing to remember is that in every experience, God allows us to learn and move and grow in our confidence. We collect confidence experience by experience.

So take out your journals, planners, Sharpies, and a big box of tissue. Let's stop gasping for air because divine confidence is already right there in you. You have everything you need.

It's time to let it out.

One

Life Is Everything You Never Thought but Always Wanted

To succeed in life, you need two things: ignorance and confidence.

—Mark Twain

It was a rainy Saturday night in Columbus, Georgia, and the auditorium was filled with more than three thousand people waiting to see their high-heeled, hair-sprayed daughters, sisters, and friends compete in the Miss Georgia pageant. It had been an incredibly long week full of rehearsals, press interviews, and workouts.

We'd competed in every category. Onstage questions, swimsuit, evening gown, talent, and the grueling five-minute interview, when five judges ask you everything from, "What is your major in college?" (mine was theology), to "What are your thoughts on climate change?" and "What do you think about the START treaty, and do you think it will be effective in limiting nuclear weapons?"

That was my actual question in the interview.

Think about it: I was nineteen years old, and with my razzle-dazzle personality, I acted much more confident than my immature mentality could back up. I certainly was not ready to pontificate about the START treaty and how it would be effective at limiting nuclear weapons.

It was the final night when the competition of seventy women was narrowed down to ten, and in about ten minutes there would be just *one*. One winner. The new Miss Georgia 1991. I had been working for a solid two years for this night, and it all boiled down to this moment.

I had so much confidence at nineteen. I was full of hope and passion for what I wanted. The dream was literally within my reach, and my preparation and path had led me to this moment. I looked at that crown, the thing that I wanted and believed I could have, but it was so much deeper; I had a clear reason for being there. It was my determined faith and belief that I could win that got me there. It was a time when I knew I was created for a life of success, excitement, achievement, and even beauty.

Fast-forward decades later, when the passion and the calling I once had was sucked out of me. Life happened. A lot of life and the belief in myself had dimmed. Where was that confident and hopeful girl now?

Can you relate? Has there been a time in your life when

you felt super excited to wake up every day? You hit the ground running with direction and excitement, and when you looked in the mirror, you liked what was staring back at you. Then the rug was yanked out from beneath you. You found yourself in a heap on the floor wondering, *Where did I go wrong?*

All my life, I've been collecting confidence through my experiences, which ultimately helped me walk in my true purpose and calling in life. I come from a place where a handshake is as binding as a contract, sweet tea is the house wine, and "y'all" is a plural pronoun. (If you really wanted to be inclusive, "all y'all" would work just fine.) One of my grandfathers was a South Carolina farmer, and the other was a preacher who could quote Genesis to Revelation—and would if you got him going. I grew up with the deep roots of family love, community strength, strong faith, and tobacco farming. This turned out to be fertile ground for collecting confidence.

This isn't some harrowing rags-to-riches story. My dad was a banker, and I had a tight-knit, loving family as I grew up in Lilburn, Georgia. Since fifth grade I lived in that village, which has a railroad that runs straight through it with trains every hour on the hour. I was a bit of an ugly duckling as a kid—my nose and mouth were bigger than most—but that didn't slow me down. My dad and I walked or jogged around nearby Stone Mountain every single day.

I was a junior in high school when I got the idea of participating in some local beauty pageants, so one day between classes I called my mom—with my last quarter, from a pay phone outside my high school cafeteria—to run the idea by her. Mom noted my short hair and said I was "out there" for the pageant world. I think she meant "out there" as a compliment and thought I might as well try. Dad wasn't too sure. "Life isn't fair," he told me. "So who knows?"

My family wasn't sure I would win, but I come from good pageant stock. My mom won many pageants and participated in Miss South Carolina. It was logical that I would follow in her high-heeled footsteps since she was my confidence coach at the time. I wasn't a textbook pageant girl (I had short hair and a big mouth and a healthy dose of delusion or confidence), but I entered several pageants. And promptly lost. However, when I was nineteen years old, I entered Miss Stone Mountain. This was a big one because winning it would qualify me for the Miss Georgia pageant. And to the surprise of my family, the audience, and myself, I won!

I was honored when I was crowned Miss Stone Mountain. For years, I'd worked for this moment—a week of rehearsals, press interviews, and workouts. But my emotional preparation really happened way before that—I was taught by strong women how to live a life of confidence.

My mother was a straight shooter who told the unvarnished truth about men, motherhood, and marriage. She was the OG (original gangster) of an empowered woman. Mom and Dad fought and complained about each other, but they were the kind of parents who—after all their fussing—will be buried in the same grave. They love well, fight well, and raised me well. Mom's always been her own person and taught me to be too.

I was always drawn to strong women like Mom.

One of these strong women was named Nancy, a painter who was somehow kin to Norman Rockwell. She knew I was interested in painting, so she let me into her life. I remember the details of one afternoon vividly. I was eight years old, and she served me fresh chocolate chip cookies in her sunroom, which was the bright color of van Gogh's *Sunflowers*. As I licked chocolate off my fingers, I watched her paint. Condensation beaded on my glass of cold milk, and perspiration formed on her forehead as the afternoon sun poured in through the glass. Her big golden retriever slept lazily at her feet. The sun was so intense, I heard the heat sizzling.

She was focused on two things: her canvas and me. For hours, we talked about everything and nothing. Spending time with her helped me excavate my talents. Watching her in the fullness of her calling was what made me want to discover my calling and develop my own gifts and talents. She painted like she was creating the *Mona Lisa*, but she was making something just for me.

She was my own Michelangelo and sculpted me in ways that would become clear as I grew older. I was mesmerized by her excellence, which was more blinding than the golden light beaming into the windows in that yellow sunroom.

And the things she painted! Once, she got out a canvas and began to apply paint with a long-handled sable bristle brush. Her strokes seemed random at first, but I was amazed as the image gradually emerged from her mind and heart and onto the canvas. It was a female mountain lion. I'd never seen her create something like that before. Southern women are more apt to paint forest scenes. Still life vases with flowers pouring out of them. Sunsets.

"It's for you," she said.

This touched me because it was so beautifully done and was painted with such love. In fact, I still have it to this day.

As I was writing this book, I thought about that painting and wished Nancy was alive so I could ask her one lingering question: *Why a female mountain lion?*

On a whim, I googled mountain lions, hoping to find some clue. And then I found it. Would you believe that a female mountain lion is called the queen?

Talk about foreshadowing!

Later, another Nancy helped shape me. She was a seventy-something-year-old widow who taught me how to sew, a huge help for my pageant outfits. After high school, in preparation for the Miss Georgia pageant, I moved in with Miss Nancy. She was my mentor and pageant director for Miss Stone Mountain. I lived in a tiny apartment above her garage.

When she talked, I listened. I hung on her every word. We'd sit and sew—me eating her amazing pimiento cheese—chatting as we worked. Once, I made a jinky-jank stitch but kept going, wanting to get it done.

"Skimp on that stitch," she said, without looking up from her fabric, "and skimp on yourself."

Shortcuts only cut yourself short.

I looked at the stitch and lamented how much time it would take to get it right. But before I started pulling the thread, she added, "Shortcuts only cut yourself short."

And I believed her. She had character under pressure and was unflappable in her confidence. She was kind and loved people as they were, not as they should be. She saw beauty in the scraps, the remnants—and she could turn them into things of beauty.

Plus, she helped me in practical ways. She and I sat at the

sewing machine and made the talent costume and swimsuit I'd wear in the competition—one perfect, loving stitch at a time.

I don't think these two Nancys ever thought they did anything out of the ordinary for me, but they did. They allowed me to observe them being authentically and confidently operational in their gifts. Pageants are about beauty, but they're about connection and confidence as well. This book is about realizing who you are—embracing your gifts and talents, the things you like to do and do well—and learning to operate and walk in confidence.

When the Miss Georgia competition finally arrived, I was swaddled in love and support from the two Nancys, my family, and my community.

"Stories like this can't come true," I had been told. But I knew different. This was my moment. I was ready for my fairy-tale ending, but I didn't try to be someone I wasn't. If I was happy, I showed that joy onstage. I patted my legs in excitement. I smiled. I waved. I was so raw, real, and naive, I didn't have any choice but to just be me. I stood in my white evening gown I'd designed in Miss Nancy's house. It had shoulder pads as wide as a lineman for the Atlanta Falcons, and I looked good. I felt good. If I won, at nineteen years old, I'd be one of the youngest winners in Miss Georgia history.

As I was standing on that big white staircase waiting to walk out on that stage for the last time, I glanced to the right. There it was: the Miss Georgia crown and sash. For a fleeting moment, I thought about grabbing it and running, but I figured out real quick my klutzy self would tumble down those majestic stairs. Instead, I leaned over and touched the crown, the thing I wanted and believed I could have. Yeah, if I won, it would mean I'd earned it. But it represented something so much deeper than winning. It was my clear purpose for being there.

For the past few years, I woke up every day ready to hit the ground running. I had direction and excitement, not to mention passion and calling. When I looked in the mirror, I liked what was staring back at me. It was a time of possibility everywhere and in everything.

"Tonight," I whispered to myself, "this crown will be mine."

The dream was literally within my reach, but I resisted the temptation to grab it. I didn't need to steal that crown. I was going to earn it.

When they began to call out the names of the runners-up, I listened carefully for my name. I didn't hear it . . . until they announced the winner of that year's Miss Georgia:

"Kim Hardee, Miss Stone Mountain."

Elated, I came down from the risers, thanked God, waved to the audience, and fought back tears. As they awarded me the crown, I tried to make myself shorter than my five-foot-eight self so they could pin it into my hair. Immediately, a song played over the loudspeakers. Not the one you can probably hum—"There She Is, Miss America"—but the state version of that, which says, "Will she be . . . Miss America?"

I enjoyed the moment, but internally I was already feeling pushed to the next thing, the next competition, the largest and most prestigious pageant in the nation: Miss America. And I'd go representing my beautiful home state of Georgia. In addition to bragging rights, Miss America is awarded scholarships, opportunities, and a national speaking tour.

I wanted that crown too.

To prepare for the Miss America pageant, I left home and went to Columbus, Georgia, where I lived with a board of advisers who were going to make sure I did everything I could to win the national title. Georgia was sweltering that summer. (This is a recurring theme for a book written by a southerner, so get ready for some sweat—or, as Julia Sugarbaker on the television show *Designing Women* would call it: "glistening.") The air was so thick you could take a bite out of it.

Come to think of it, air had just about the number of calories I was allowed to eat between then and the pageant. In just a few short months, I'd be strutting my stuff in a swimsuit in front of judges, and they'd look at every inch of me. And I was already taller and curvier than my predecessor, which my new advisers noticed after looking me up and down.

After a few minutes of casual chitchat with these two strangers with whom I'd live for the next few months, one made a suggestion: "Don't say 'ain't.' We need to clean up your language if you want to compete on a national scale."

Like most southern people, I grew up with language that might not be grammatically correct but gets the point across. My conversation was frequently enhanced with such sayings as "She's nicer than a buttered biscuit" or "She's nuttier than a squirrel turd." That's the way we talked.

"Colloquialisms might be considered charming back home," she said. "But they won't work at Miss America. We want you to appear as educated as the others."

As the others?

I was now barely twenty years old, so I had attained as much education as anyone needs at that age. But the idea that I was "less than" took hold of me. In the past, I'd competed against myself—always trying to do better than my previous performances. I wanted to be the best me I could be. But now I was pitted against the other women, looking at them, assessing them, feeling that I was simply less than what they had achieved. Comparison, the ultimate confidence killer, was a bad habit that stuck with me for decades. And at this pageant level, it was all about presenting yourself in a certain way—not in an authentic way but in a fake-as-all-get-out way.

> Comparison, the ultimate confidence killer, is a bad habit that can stick with you for life.

Everything in my guts rebelled against this, but I wanted to please them, so I just nodded. These experts knew more than I did, right?

Has this happened to you?

I'm sure you can remember a moment when you compromised who you are—knowing it was wrong but you did it anyway—assuming the experts knew better? I thought so.

"Also, we're going to change your clothes," the other adviser said. "We're going to hire designers and professionals to make your competition wardrobe."

I thought about Miss Nancy with her thread and needles, the love that had been sewn into every inch of my outfits back home. I felt a pang. But again, I went along with it.

"Who am I supposed to be?" I tried to keep the tremble out of my voice.

"For one thing, be quieter," the pageant adviser said. "For the Miss America pageant, you're going to present yourself in a different way than you presented yourself at Miss Georgia.

From now on, don't slap your leg. Don't smile like you just heard a joke. Just tone it down a bit."

My advisers were educators—they were good-hearted people. Really intelligent. If I saw them today, I'd want to kiss them on the face.

But the advice they were giving me was not *for* me. They'd never dealt with a contestant like me. Mom was right when she called me "out there" for a pageant contestant. I needed to be me. I needed to express myself in the way that was most natural to me. The way God made me. My advisers weren't the enemy. In fact, they were right in so many ways. I was fighting against myself. But at the time, I was perfectly willing to listen to their advice and take it, even though it felt off.

Every day for about three months, it was the same. I'd get up, work out, read the paper, catch up on current events, do mock interviews, rehearse, and go to bed. I was doing all the right things outwardly, but inside I was having a crisis of confidence.

I didn't know how to fix that.

So I spent a lot of time wishing I could recreate that loving atmosphere back in my painter friend Nancy's sunroom, with her freshly baked cookies on a plate next to a glass of milk. I didn't have Nancy, so Piggly Wiggly cupcakes had to do. During the days, I'd secretly buy a package of six cupcakes (chocolate with white icing!) and keep them under my bed. I'd take out a cupcake, take a bite, and let its sweet goodness wash over me before hiding it under the bed.

It tasted like home.

I've had a lot of good friends over the years, but I'm not

sure I've ever had a BFF as comforting as those cupcakes were back then.

Then one day, my pageant advisers discovered my cupcake stash and tossed them unceremoniously into the garbage can. My heart sank as I watched them disappear into the trash.

"I want to come home," I said to my mom over the phone, fighting back tears. But we both knew I couldn't give up this opportunity. So I continued to live with the advisers, allowing them to take "the Kim" out of me.

I felt so alone.

That fall when I traveled from Columbus, Georgia, to Atlantic City to participate in the Miss America pageant, I felt ill-prepared, confused, exhausted, and mentally weak. I'd worked out so much, my body was perfect, especially since my cupcakes had been confiscated.

But I questioned my own being.

The competition began, whether I was ready for it or not. Preliminary competitions lasted four days, as the women were judged and measured against each other. One evening after a day of hard competition, I was in my hotel room in Atlantic City. I was feeling listless. Not myself.

That's when the phone rang in my room. I jumped. We weren't supposed to have any contact with the outside world. I wasn't supposed to call my mom, but I snuck in a call because I had to speak to her. When I picked up the receiver, the caller identified herself as Lauren Green. She was the first African American winner of the Miss Minnesota pageant in 1984, was third runner-up in the Miss America pageant of 1985, and had judged me at the Miss Georgia pageant.

I didn't know her, but she'd been a judge at the statewide

pageant. She had seen the real me, and she was calling to ask why I wasn't being myself—the same Kim she picked to be Miss Georgia.

"Kim, where are you?" she asked. "What's happened?"

I was stunned. I had just turned twenty a little over a month before, and I was simply trying to live up to the Miss America standards. But looking back, I'd been handled, managed, and coached right out of myself to the extent that I didn't know how to respond to what she was asking.

Finally, the last night of the competition arrived, broadcast on NBC with hosts Regis Philbin and Kathie Lee Gifford. Donald Trump and Marla Maples sat on the front row, watching along with millions of Americans, including the Nancys and my family back home. We contestants had a chance to introduce ourselves to the nation. My big moment had arrived—but it felt empty and false. Then we did a group performance dressed all in white, but I felt awkward. Self-conscious. Not myself. I just wasn't feeling it.

To save time, the rest of the broadcast would focus on the top ten contestants. Regis announced the names with his typical dramatic flair. Just as I'd done at the Miss Georgia contest, I waited to hear my name, but this time it wasn't called.

I probably wouldn't have recognized it anyway.

There I stood on that stage. Defeated. I'd lost pageants before. But I'd never lost myself.

That was one of my life's turning points. I'm sure you've had yours—perhaps less public but perhaps just as painful. I gave it everything—I mean, everything I knew to give—and still felt as if I'd just gotten a mammogram while everyone was watching.

I did everything I was told to do. I gave all my time, focus, energy, sweat, and tears. I even gave up cupcakes, and I worked out like a fiend! I gave everything I had to give at that time and came up wanting. I felt as if I'd lost the permission to be my true self. I'd lost my confidence—or doubted whether I ever really had any.

I know pageant-angst is probably not on your top-ten list of things to be worried about. Me either. But I wrote this book because I believe many of you might feel the same way. Your heart has been broken by a million of life's disappointments, just as mine was, and you're trying to put it back together again.

My heart was broken.

At least for a time.

But I am here to tell you if someone had given me some warning about the things that have happened in my life, I would have bought stock in Amazon and skipped the down-and-outs, the failures, and even a near-death experience. But each one has guided me to where I am now. This life is everything I never thought but always wanted. I've never met a strong person with an easy past.

Now you might be asking, "Kim, what makes your book so different?" or you may be asking "Where are my car keys?" (Did you check the fridge? True story.) This book is different because I'm going to give you the answer right here in the first chapter. Usually, you have to read the whole book to find out what it's all about, like there are many paths to purpose, and it's all in your head and you've had the power all along . . . *blah blah blah*.

But actually, that part is right. Not the *blah blah blah* part (the title of my next book?). The part that says, "You've had the power all along." That's right.

Here's the truth. Every story, every memory of your life plays a part in fashioning the design that is your calling, and what you were fashioned for is greatness. God knitted you together in your mother's womb. It says so right in Psalms, along with the revelation that you are "fearfully and wonderfully made": "For you formed my inward parts; you knitted me together in my mother's womb. I praise you, for I am fearfully and wonderfully made. Wonderful are your works; my soul knows it very well" (Psalm 139:13–14 ESV).

Sometimes that verse is printed on birth announcements in frilly font, but you don't outgrow God's plan for your life, and I want you to hear it in all caps. You're the same person you were before the doctor slapped you on the behind. The substance of who you are and who you're going to be now was designed before the first moment you entered the earth. God sat there and lovingly created you, just like Nancy and I fashioned my shoulder-padded evening gown. Except you're even better than that gown, which might go in and out of style. (Hot take: shoulder pads should make a comeback along with wooden heel Candie's!)

I know what it's like to make fashion. I struggle to create forty new styles every month, let alone making billions of people on the planet. It's so hard to come up with something creative and unique, but God pulled it off with you. You have characteristics, insights, and experiences that no one else on the planet has or ever had. Some of those experiences have been good, and some of them have been bad.

The substance of who you are and who you're going to be now was designed before the first moment you entered the earth.

But let's get away from the shame, stereotypes, and labels. I'm not even talking about that stuff. I'm talking about the deep, real, and mysterious components of *you* that never existed before in the history of the earth until now. And yet, here you are, reading this book, acting like you're not much to brag about.

The mold was broken—heck, there wasn't even a mold to begin with—when God fashioned you and knitted you together. It took me a while to understand the implications of this mystery, and I have to remind myself every day.

If you're like me, you need a little gentle—and sometimes not-so-gentle—pep talk about who you were designed to be. That's where this book comes in.

Let's face it. When the doctor slapped our backsides when we were born, it wasn't the last slap life gave us. So pour some coffee and go grab some cupcakes from Piggly Wiggly in honor of the good things that life has taken away from us.

Turn the page if you want to get them back.

Two

If You Ain't Dead, You Ain't Done!

Sometimes a storm in your life is what will blow you to the place you are longing to be.

—Beth Moore

I had prepared for the pageant, but not for my life.

After I lost the Miss America pageant, there was nowhere else to go. I'd competed at the highest pageant level and lost. My lifelong dreams were no longer gettable, like the box of cereal too high on the grocery store shelf.

Out of reach.

Time to move on.

But I no longer believed anything I used to believe about myself. I didn't believe I had talent, anything unique about me, or an interesting point of view. I'd lost control of my life and didn't have a map or GPS.

So I did what I thought everyone expected me to do. The cultural default mode for me in my early twenties, especially back then, was obvious. I was supposed to fall in love, get married, have kids, and paint the picket fence white.

Little did I know, you can't pattern your life after a Hallmark movie.

One evening, when I was twenty-one years old, I got a gig singing in a local nightclub. I was soulfully singing Aretha Franklin and Etta James songs with a full house band when I noticed the owner watching me from the back of the club. He looked more like a bouncer. Maybe he was about ten years older than I was. He was tall with dark hair and a muscular build. Quick smile.

Girl, I melted.

We started dating, and I played a part: the sweet little submissive woman who'd be a great, quiet wife. (Okay, stop laughing. Really. Stop.)

After a whirlwind romance, he proposed, and I said yes. We told my parents while sitting at their kitchen table.

"Are you an idiot, Kim? This is the biggest mistake of your life," Mom said. She knew the relationship wasn't right. He was like a wild horse that could never be tamed.

"Do what you want," she said to him, "but she'll never stay with you."

You'd think this would've slowed my roll, but it didn't. I went into planning mode, focusing more on the wedding than the actual marriage.

I had a stunning dress that looked like Cinderella had

walked through an explosion at the sequin factory. America had a tulle shortage that year because my veil used every yard. Plus, my bouquet was bigger than my body.

The marriage might not have looked good to my friends and family, but the wedding sure did.

The fantasy world I'd been concocting disappeared the moment I placed my foot in the aisle. I looked at my white satin shoe. It felt like lead.

I was making a mistake, but I couldn't turn back now. It was too late. I was too far gone. So I placed one foot down, then the other, marching slowly down the wrong path. I said the vows and drank the Kool-Aid, but I was as fake as the pearls around my neck.

After the wedding, things began to unravel. I won't go into all the details, but he was wild as a buck. He never pretended to be otherwise, but it felt different once we were married. I couldn't live like that.

Okay, I'll be real with you. It wasn't *totally* his fault. I was the faker, not him. He was the same guy the whole way through. He married me because of what I was pretending to be. (That sound you hear is my mama somewhere in Atlanta yelling, "I told you so!" But ignore her. This is just you and me.)

I'm just trying to say that I don't blame him for any of this. When things go wrong, we want to blame everyone: our ex, our boss, our parents, and even the mailman. But I had to own my junk, and I had more than Fred Sanford.

Two years later, I left.

As a married couple, we didn't have much, other than a red Ford pickup in my name, which would get "repoed" if I left it up to him to pay its monthly bill.

I kept it.

"I don't want you driving around in a pickup truck," my dad told me. He bought my mom a new car every two years and hated the thought of me tooling around town in such a masculine ride, especially since he'd bought me a new silver Firebird when I was in high school. This ride seemed like a downgrade to him, but I had no choice.

After a quick search, I got a job leasing apartments at a complex on Jimmy Carter Boulevard in Metro Atlanta, situated on a street full of strip malls, tattoo parlors, no-tell motels, and cheaply constructed buildings. As an employee, the owner gave me a discount on a lease.

When I moved in, I stood back and marveled: my whole life fit into a small U-Haul trailer. Alone, I began to unpack. The tears I was crying must've blinded my vision, because when I unpacked a wedding gift—an expensive vase—I dropped it and watched it break into a thousand pieces. That's how my heart felt. Shattered. Hopeless. Weary. Weighed down.

Still, I did what I had to do—I swept it up and tried to make a home. I didn't have much to work with. My new place had a small bedroom, dingy carpet, walls thinner than water, and carpet in the bathroom. But it also had a dining room, sunroom, fireplace, and a beautiful, wooded view.

Dad didn't see its attributes. When he came over for the first time, he frowned. He wasn't the stereotypical protective dad who tried to clean up my messes. He always empowered me to protect myself. Even though my parents ended up with a country club life, they built everything they had from the ground up. They knew I'd made my bed and had to lie in it. Though this life wasn't what Dad had envisioned for me—and he knew it wasn't what I envisioned for myself—dreaming was over. This was just straight-up survival.

I'd ruined my life and needed to figure out plan B.

"What are people gonna think about me?" I cried to him as we stood in that apartment. "Everyone came to the wedding, and now . . ."

"Kim, I have some news for you." He stopped me right there. "They're not thinking about you at all. They're thinking about themselves."

He was right.

This dingy, seedy apartment was a physical reminder of the mess I'd made of my own life, but I was determined to make a palace out of that place. I tried to make it reflect my true self.

Who was my true self? I didn't know anymore. No idea. Surely to goodness, not this.

I got cleaning supplies. I scrubbed, vacuumed, and cleaned that apartment until it sparkled like Prince Charming's teeth.

First, I painted the boring tan walls pink. Think Pepto Bismol. My neighbor (who was single and recently divorced too) came over to help me. She painted the walls, and I handled the trim. Then I got a white couch, a shower curtain with big pink flowers on it, and a rug to cover up the dingy carpet. I went to a furniture rental place that had old stuff they couldn't rent anymore. There, I found a gorgeous white lacquer dining room set, on which I applied white nail polish to cover most of the nicks and dings. I bought dishes from the grocery store and hung pictures on the wall—think 1980s, art deco Duran Duran album cover–type art. When I was finished—paint splatters dried on my sweatpants—I looked around. *That's more like it.*

Dad called every morning at six o'clock on the way to work. He was my therapist, my life coach before life coaches were a thing. He would say, "It's just so hard for me to watch you go through this." He knew I needed to figure out what went wrong.

Even trying to figure it out was exhausting. I tried to stay busy so I wouldn't feel that regret and exhaustion, but the loneliness outpaced my busyness.

It caught up with me.

I read a lot of books at night. Sometimes I'd just sit in silence and think about how everyone had been right—I wasn't enough. I was a piece of junk.

One evening I cried out, *God, where are You? Am I enough?*

To my astonishment, He spoke back in a small, still voice.

And since I had nothing else to do and nowhere else to go, I listened.

I've got you. Are you ready for what I really have for you? It's not for the fainthearted. Lean in. Hush and listen. Do nothing. I'll bring you what you need. Stop flailing. It's just Me and you.

God didn't give me a to-do list, and He wasn't breaking me down and starting from scratch. He was positioning me for my calling. That was it.

I was twenty-three years old and already divorced. I felt like a failure. It was so painful and hard, but looking back, it was difficult in the best kind of way. I had nothing to lose and everything to gain. When life puts you in a position of pause, it can be exciting. I was alone with my thoughts—a dangerous place to be—and I decided to get to know God more. My grandfather was a preacher, but in this moment, I realized I needed my own faith, not the borrowed kind passed down for generations.

I opened my Bible and drank it in. The Scripture jumped off the page and slapped me in my face. It was so real. But not only did it challenge me, it comforted me every day.

And so did my dad. He showed up at my apartment one day holding a picture.

"What'd you bring me?" I asked.

"A picture of you," he said as he handed it to me. To my surprise, it wasn't some childhood photo of me eating birthday cake or riding a tricycle.

"This is a seagull eating a frog," I said. *Had he lost it?*

"Look close." He smiled. The head of the frog was in the seagull's mouth but the frog—with his little hands still free—was choking the seagull. Outmatched, he refused to relent to the jaws of defeat.

"You're this one," he said, pointing to the frog. "Never give up."

This stuck in my craw, but in a good way. As I held that frog picture, I accepted the fact that life is 89.5 percent hard, and the rest is pretty good. It's not going to be easy, but I was going to try to be like that frog. Life is hard, God is good, and people are crazy (me included). When I figured that out, the right opportunities emerged. How quickly we go from being on top to not. Just two short years ago from competing in Miss America to sitting alone, divorced, in a one-bedroom apartment on Jimmy Carter Boulevard.

A few weeks later, my phone rang. "Can you come sing at our event?" There's nothing like being broke to make you appreciate an offer like that. Honey, I couldn't say yes fast enough. I would've sung at the grocery store.

I wasn't hustling and trying to force anything. I was just accepting what came my way, no matter how small.

I just sat still and let go of the anxiety. I didn't force it. I also didn't get attached to what success should look like. I just walked through the doors that opened.

What else was I going to do?

Slowly, day by day, through drawing closer to God and having long talks with my dad, I began to remember I was enough. More than enough. It was hard to believe, but that door was slightly cracked open, and I began to see into a better existence, just waiting for me. Could it be true? I wasn't convinced, but I felt God's affection. And it was hopeful and comfortable, like a cozy blanket on a dark, winter's night.

I wrapped God's love around me, pulled it up to my chin, and nestled into its warmth.

We're always collecting something as we travel along life's road—pain, bitterness, sorrows. But during this time, I began collecting confidence again. It took chipping away all those extraneous things for me to find what really mattered. Tough stuff does that. I am hardheaded, and maybe I needed extra time to understand what I was called to do.

I started to exchange the shame of my divorce for the strength of my testimony. I turned around my self-absorbed "Why me?" attitude and started being grateful for even the smallest blessings that came my way. I became grateful for all the time I spent alone working on myself because I was developing my relationship with God. I started looking at my past failures as preparing me for something bigger.

I'd gone down to the bottom of the barrel (at least as far down as I could've gone at that age), because I was divorced at twenty-three and I had to bring a calculator to the grocery store just to make sure my check didn't bounce. More than once, I had to put the box of Cheerios back on the shelf. I'd gone from what seemed like a pinnacle to an old beat-up pick-up truck and furniture painted with nail polish. I knew *why* I'd gone through all of this turmoil at such a young age—you can't make as many bad decisions as I had and then act surprised when it all unravels.

But through all the struggles, I began to understand the "why" of my life.

You can use your dark moments to understand your "whys" as well.

Do you believe everyone has a calling?

I've traveled the world and asked audiences if they believe that people have a calling. Without fail, every hand goes up. But when I ask how many are living their life's calling, cue the crickets.

We can't just ignore the question, like a calculus problem too hard to figure out. We think of calling as external. But just like in those horror movies, the call is coming from inside the house. It's internal. That's what haunts us. Our calling is haunting us because we know we have a big one, but we can't seem to put our finger on it. The lack of knowing your calling might manifest differently in your life.

Do you ever say things like these?

"I'm just so tired."

"If I could just lose twenty pounds . . . "

"I'm just a housewife."

"If I could just figure out what I want to do . . . "

These chats start with "just" and end with "what's wrong with me?" What they're really asking is, "What's my calling?"

It might seem mysterious and impossible, but I began to ask, to search, to beg for understanding. I was flat on my face before God month after month, asking, "Why am I on this planet?"

Then, like Arnold Horshack from the TV show *Welcome Back, Kotter,* my calling raised its hand and got my attention. When I acknowledged it, the answer spilled out.

To my surprise, I already knew it.

When I was a kid, I was convinced I was created to sing and talk. I used to line up my dolls, grab a hairbrush microphone, and perform a concert worthy of Carnegie Hall. I sang to my toys, I sang at church, I sang to anyone who'd stand still long enough for me to finish a song. My first singing gig was at a local preliminary WWF wrestling match at Brookwood High School when I was ten years old. I walked out there with my plaid skirt and argyle socks, carrying a boombox and listening to the instrumental version of "Angels Watching Over Me" by Amy Grant. I was scared half to death—I even peed on myself a little bit—but, honey, I belted out that song to all those down-home, tatted wrestling fans.

Back then, I knew why I was created. But life beat it out of me. Heck, maybe I just got distracted by that sexy night club owner.

And there it was, right there again. Familiar. Smiling. *Hey, it's me again.*

But my calling in life was not an occupation. It was a vocation. Maybe you've heard people use "occupation" and "vocation" interchangeably, but they are not the same. An occupation is what you decide to do. A vocation is following a voice. The Latin word *vocare* means "to call," and God is the One who calls.

In my occupation, I could be a professional singer or communicator, sure. Just like you might be an accountant, a nurse, or a schoolteacher. But our jobs are just the setting for our callings. As Dr. Dan Allender, the renowned therapist, wrote, "Our calling is not what we do—but how we do it."[1] I'm not talking about what you fill out on a form on the blank that says "work." I'm talking about vocation, which is more divine, more exciting. Having said that, a person's calling is usually short enough to fit in a blank. Usually, it's one or two words.

By now we're friends, so I'll go ahead and tell you mine: edification. That's a ten-gallon word for "building up." You know you've found your calling when it not only helps you but also spills over to others around you in service. Self-help is fine, but helping others is power.

Self-help is fine, but helping others is power.

I accomplish my calling of the edification of others through my singing and talking, but I also do it with my fashion and cosmetic lines. I'm trying to do it with this book too. In fact, I don't do anything without the express purpose of building up those around me.

Nothing.

That simplifies life.

Did my childhood self know that? No. But my calling had been speaking to me for years, gently giving me hints, hoping

I'd one day sit down at that white table in my first apartment on Jimmy Carter Boulevard and put the pieces of the puzzle together, so I could finally see the picture emerge.

Your calling (and you have a *big* one) is the common thread sewn in your life story and it's always knocking at your door. We take it for granted. We think, *Oh, that's nothing special because it comes easy and natural for me.* But pay attention to what causes you joy because it'll give you uncommon energy.

It'll surprise you.

You don't have to chase your calling by looking for it, trying to create it, or conjuring it up from nothing. You don't play Whac-A-Mole with it. It doesn't pop up randomly and then disappear if you don't pounce quickly enough.

Your calling chases you.

Sit back, put down your mallet, and watch.

You are where you need to be.

When I turned on the television in that apartment on Jimmy Carter Boulevard, it'd always start on WATC, channel 2. To call it a community channel was an understatement. It was small. Homemade. People from Atlanta just got on there and talked about whatever was on their mind.

I could do that.

I called the number on TV to apply for a interview on their show. They sent me an application and booked me. Imagine my surprise when I looked at the address of the station: it was two blocks from my apartment.

The same street.

God had been positioning me the whole time. I didn't have

a road map, but I did, it turns out, have GPS: God's Positioning System. That's all you need.

It was a simple segment. In my segment, I told them how I was a former Miss Georgia, a failed Miss America contestant, and a recent divorcée.

Nice résumé, huh?

Then I sang.

"Does the place you're called to labor seem too small and little known?" I gave it all I had, and the words meant so much. Especially the next words, which came in the chorus: "Little is much when God is in it, labor not for wealth or fame; there's a crown, and you can win it."[2]

A crown I could win? Count me in. This local gig wasn't broadcast to the nation—and, no, Johnny Carson didn't hit me up afterward. But I got my own weekly talk show because I was available and lived close to the station. It was called *Friends & Neighbors,* and it lasted for ten years.

During my dark days, when I was devastated and thought I'd ruined my life, those broken pieces were being formed into my future. During that time, I cut my very first solo independent album. I was like MC Hammer hocking those CDs out of the back of my truck. The creativity, ingenuity, toughness, and mental stability required to make music and have a talk show came from that time alone. I would not be in TV, have the career I have today, or be writing this book if I hadn't been in that Pepto Bismol pink apartment located on the same street as the tv station WATC.

A place or circumstance can put you on a collision path with your calling. I mean that literally. Not until I sat down to write this book did I realize the significance of that apartment being on the very street as my calling.

You're surrounded by signs. Look up. Notice it. Be ready for miracles. It's right in front of your face.

Yes, even if you screwed up and you're somewhere you never thought you'd be. You are there for a reason. But you don't have to be there forever.

It's time for some faith to kick in, give up what you thought life should look like, and let go of control. Honey, I'll tell you right now: you never had control anyway.

We think we do, which leads us to believe we've blown it.

Well, this ain't about what you have or have not done. God is the master of the universe, not you. You couldn't fix your mistakes if you tried. So quit worrying about it. Nobody really cares about your screwups. Like my dad said, they aren't even thinking about you anyway.

You might be out there trying to get over your past, hard times, and struggles, not realizing all of that is locked into your calling. There's a "why" you went through that. But we get hung up on what happened *to* us instead of what can happen *through* us. We try to rush through our problems, to shorten our dark days, and try to find a solution to our sorrow as soon as possible. We're not still enough or quiet enough or willing to seek Him enough to let Him do what He can do. And Ephesians 3:20 says He "is able to do immeasurably more than

We get hung up on what happened *to* us instead of what can happen *through* us.

all we ask or imagine, according to his power that is at work within us."

We all have our dark nights of the soul. Those moments in our lives where everything seems covered up by pain and hopelessness. They can be the true compass to our calling if we listen to what they are trying to tell us. We don't value them, don't want to go through them, or we do the easy thing to distract ourselves—with Instagram, reality TV (which I love), and TikTok. (My distraction is the "Add to Cart" button.) We don't take time to slow down and just go through the experience of pain, to reflect about what we really want, and to listen to that still, small voice. But those are the most prosperous moments that can ever be given—if you're quiet enough, still enough, or willing enough to listen to them. This divorce was the most authentic, raw time of my life thus far. You can't be authentic in the world if you can't be real with yourself.

You can't be authentic in the world if you can't be real with yourself.

I let the waves of pain wash over me. And they lifted me like a tide lifts a ship.

Your mistakes are not wasted.

The mistake is the steak. It's the meat and potatoes. That's the good stuff. Don't rush this feast. Relish every bite.

I want you to live your passion.

When it comes to dress or pant size, I'm a tight 12 and a loose 14. That's okay for clothing, but no one wants a life that's ill-fitting. You want to live a life that's custom-made, designed to fit you perfectly. Sadly, too many people are trying to fit into a life they outgrew years ago. I did this *big time.* We keep having the same tired conversations with ourselves and others when our hearts know we were meant for greater things. Now is the right time to do and be and talk about greater things.

When you're operating in your calling, confidence comes. It feels like home. And there is no mortgage, no interest rate, and it's free. It was a gift given to you in your mother's womb. By God. At the beginning of time. The only thing you have to figure out is what you're passionate about and do it. If you're not passionate, it'll be stale. It won't be authentic. It won't be true. That's everything.

Here's a little controversy, mama bears.

I ask women, "What are you called to do?"

Invariably someone responds, "To be a wife." Usually followed by, "I'm meant to be a mom."

Nope.

Your purpose was *not* to get married and have children. Marriage and kids are fantastic. I love my children, and parenting is my biggest responsibility right now. Giving birth or adopting is a blessing! It's your most important job and it goes so fast. Slowing down to raise your kids is important.

It might feel like you'll forever be changing diapers, driving carpool, and sitting in uncomfortable bleachers yelling at your kids to get that rebound.

You won't. My sons will always be my babies, but they'll only be living under my roof for a season. Do the math. If you live until you're ninety, your kids will usually be at home for only 20 percent of your life.

It's a short amount of time. What are you gonna do with the rest of your time?

The best thing we can do for our children is to live our calling. Parenting is more about who you are than about what you do or say. We are our calling and living that out will set them on their own path to calling.

When I was a little girl and started to get glimpses of what my life might be, I was usually alone—sitting quietly playing with my dolls or walking to school. Things were quiet enough for me to notice that still, small voice.

I did have a big advantage over some of you young'uns. I didn't have an iPhone, a console, or an iPad to distract me. It was just me, Strawberry Shortcake, and Shaun Cassidy looking down at me from a poster on the wall.

When I was home, I was home, and I could just be me. I could play and get dirty, and it didn't matter. When I hit my teens, if I had a big ole zit right on my forehead, I didn't care, and no one else did either.

When I was growing up, I could freely be me—flaws and all—but social media has burst that bubble. The pressure to be perfect has infiltrated the four walls of our homes. Now, even if you're lying on your couch, you can compare your butt to Kim Kardashian's (and she has a *killer* booty!), see the exotic vacations of your neighbors, and feel less important than everyone else. But 99.9 percent of people you see online have lives that aren't as sparkly without the filter. Confession: this includes me. I edit my photos, but I'm real enough to admit it. Sometimes optics can help a girl out, but optics aren't power. True power comes from a place you cannot see in a photo, even with the best Instagram filter.

I'm not blaming social media; I'm on every platform. But it is harder than ever to be present in the moment. So turn off your apps, sit still, get quiet, and be willing to pay attention to what's going on inside you.

YOUR CALLING IS PERSONAL

You're called to be you! And your calling is aligned with your personality, talent, and era. God created you at this specific time, with your specific gifts and talents. In this book, I want to encourage you to use what you've got!

You're called to be you!

We're taught that we have to measure our worth and consequence immediately—by the number of digits in our bank account, the number of likes we have on our social posts, or the number of steps taken on those pesky health apps. (*Wait! I've only taken thirty-seven steps today? There must be something wrong with my tech!*)

Life doesn't work that way. We can't measure our worth by numbers. You are priceless, even if it looks like your impact is small.

Don't despise small beginnings because we can't do what we're not called to do. We're supposed to teach our children how to live so that wisdom is passed down through generations. But they can't do our work, and we can't do theirs.

Even if it seems you share the same calling with another person, it will manifest in different ways, present different challenges, and offer different payoffs. But living in your calling is reward enough because it multiplies. The more you operate in this place of calling, the more your opportunities, platforms, resources, and joy (and just everything else) multiplies. Yes, in this lifetime. It not only creates a legacy, but you reap *huge* benefits in the *now*.

When you finally give up your illusion of control and lean into your calling, God gives extravagantly in ways you can't imagine—with results that last.

YOUR CALLING IS PROLIFIC

There's an old saying that goes like this: "You can count the seeds in an apple, but you can't count the apples in a seed." The more you plant, the more you harvest. But walking in your true calling produces much fruit and has a lot of offspring.

Some of the fruit isn't good. Some of the harvest doesn't come as you'd hoped. But, even in that, your harvest is bountiful, and it takes time to grow. It also multiplies in ways you won't be able to see immediately.

Case in point. In Germany, twenty thousand people per day visit one of the most famous tourist sites: the Cologne Cathedral. The first stone of the building, created to provide a final resting place for the remains of the three wise men in the Bible story of Christmas, was laid in 1248 . . . and it wasn't completed for 632 years![3]

I get antsy when a bathroom remodel takes a few months.

However, these cathedral builders were willing to start a project, do their part, and trust that the work would be completed. Not by their kids or their grandchildren, or even their grandchildren's grandchildren . . . and their work still creates awe in camera-toting tourists today.

The cathedral bricklayers who worked over the six centuries had the same overall purpose, but each was called to a different stage of the process, which came with its own challenges and opportunities. The bricklayers in 1248 Cologne could lay only the first stones. I bet some of them felt a sense of hopelessness without knowing the end result. Maybe others were determined. The 1880 bricklayers who completed the cathedral—a day that became a national holiday—didn't have the vision to lay the first stone but got to enjoy the celebration.

Your calling resides in perpetuity and does not obey your self-imposed timetable.

Your calling resides in perpetuity and does not obey your self-imposed timetable. To paraphrase Gandalf in *The Fellowship of the Ring,* calling is never late nor early. It operates precisely when it means to.

YOUR CALLING NEVER EXPIRES

I could've done anything in my twenties, but I followed a pattern. Instead of doing what I thought the culture wanted me to do, I should've figured out my calling.

That's what happened during my time alone in my apartment, and it changed my life. The beautiful thing is that you can do this at any age. The world will tell you that you can only answer your calling when you're young, but it isn't like the chunky milk in the back of the fridge. It doesn't expire.

I've always loved to be around older women, breathing in their wisdom. My mother, who is now in her seventies, is living her best life. Suddenly, she's modeling on national television! While most people don't get to reinvent themselves as models, I've had dozens of mentors in my life—women (and a few men)—who had cool hobbies, and those who didn't. They didn't tell me how to live; they modeled character and integrity.

The world tells us our calling presents itself during a small window of time. One strike, and you're out. You might think you had one chance to accomplish your dreams and let it slip through your fingers.

You have not. God finishes what He starts.

Your calling reveals itself gradually as you can handle it. Pay attention to the miracles around you.

I now have a business with more than two hundred-million-dollars in sales, but sometimes I long for those times in that Pepto Bismol–pink apartment. Ain't that funny? I'd give anything to be alone there right now with a full day, just to cry it out alone with my thoughts. I'd love to have my neighbor pop in and help me paint sloppily.

> Pay attention to the miracles around you.

Those years are right up there with the births of my children. Looking back, that time of angst was one of my happiest and most important times. I was on my own, and as I spent more time reading my Bible and spending time with my heavenly Father and my earthly one, eventually I felt the same jolt of joy I experienced when I jumped the fence and walked to elementary school all by myself. I stood on my own two feet. I would not be here if I'd not been there.

Speaking of feet, look down at your own. Are you on the right path?

If not, I'm here to tell you that it's not too late for you to pick a new path. You have to start where you are to get where you want to be. Your feet might feel like lead. You might be either too afraid or too tired to take a step in a new direction, but take a moment to pause. You might be in a terrible place, but I challenge you to see the beauty around you. Your place of regret is also a place of enormous hope and opportunity.

So go ahead, pick up your foot, and turn yourself in the right direction. You don't have to figure out your whole life to start living in your calling.

Because if you ain't dead, you ain't done.

The Calling Credo

KIM GRAVEL

1. I trust that my calling is not a *what* but a *why*.
2. I trust that my calling will come from a common thread of joy in my life.
3. I trust my biggest fears and insecurities will point me toward my calling.
4. I trust that no matter what age or what stage of life I'm in, now's the time to live out God's calling for my life.
5. I trust that I wasn't put here on earth just to take up space, but to make a difference.
6. I trust that God is a lamp unto my feet and will light my path.
7. I trust that I already have the gifts and talents to fulfill my calling.
8. I trust that I can start where I am now and become who I am meant to be.

Three

Don't Edit Your Story

From the time I was a kid, I always knew something was going to happen to me. Didn't know exactly what.

—Elvis Presley

I belted out Whitney Houston's song "How Will I Know?" as I tooled around the house, wondering whether someone *really* loved me. I was obsessed with Whitney, but my younger sister Allisyn poured water all over my fun.

"He'll call you," she said. "That's how you'll know!"

I rolled my eyes. I wasn't interested in the game of romance. After getting divorced at twenty-three, I was done. I liked to date, but I wasn't interested in uprooting my life for the sake of love. Been there, done that. To be honest, I was ashamed of being divorced. At that time, it was the first divorce in my family. Isn't it strange how we attach shame to just about every mistake we make? I've spent a lot of time pondering shame and why it comes so easy to us, or at least to me. Is it because we are so performance driven, or are we as humans always striving for perfection?

My shame came from the mistake I made getting married and then quickly divorced. I developed a deep-seated fear of failure, especially when it came to romantic relationships. When I made a mistake or experienced failure, I anticipated shame would follow.

But I loved to sing, so I created my first album with money I earned as a supervisor of an apartment complex. I called the album *For the First Time.* My original title song included the lyrics, "For the first time, I'm picking up the pieces . . . for the first time, I'm feeling happy about myself."[1] That nicely summed up where I was. I know those weren't revolutionary set-the-world-on-fire lyrics, but breaking through the low moments and finally feeling happy about myself at that time felt so good.

To promote the album, I sang at Roswell Street Baptist Church in Marietta, Georgia, and I was invited to a retreat. When I went to the worship leader's home to discuss the details of the gig, I noticed a woman sitting on the floor painting cabinets. Her hair was curly—think 1990s-era Nicole Kidman.

I was technically on the job, but I wasn't performing. I was in planning mode, so I wasn't looking fabulous with a face full of makeup and decked out in high heels. I looked like a ragamuffin—no cosmetics, probably no bra. I could tell the girl with the curly hair was taken aback by my ramshackle appearance, and I was taken by how pretty she was.

"You look like a mermaid," I said, admiring the woman's long red hair.

"Well, you look like Princess Diana," she said, noting my short blonde hair.

To quote from *Jerry Maguire,* she "had me at hello"![2] She told me her name was Amy, and I liked her from the get-go, but Amy didn't like me at first. After seeing me perform, she assumed I'd be stuck-up and arrogant—perhaps people think pageant winners are naturally uppity.

Amy was the most authentic, genuine person I've ever met, and we became roommates.

We became fast friends, best friends. I would even say kindred spirits, just like Anne Shirley and Diana Barry from *Anne of Green Gables.* Amy was a singer and songwriter, and we hit it off creatively. The number one thing we had in common: we were both single. But, unlike Amy, I wasn't ready to mingle.

A part of me still carried shame about my divorce. That's the way I am, and maybe you are too. Even though I knew—in my head—that I made the right decision to leave my first husband, another part of me knew that I'd made the totally wrong decision in marrying him in the first place. But life, like many songs, is sometimes aspirational.

To promote the album, I transformed myself into a kind of "Gospel Whitney Houston" and set out on a church tour. Because I'd been Miss Georgia, I was well known in my local area because I'd served in various capacities at various events. There's nothing like going to the Gwinnett County

Fairgrounds, being the grand marshal of the Snellville Days Parade, and judging the pageant for Rattlesnake Roundup Queen! (I bet Whitney never did that!) However, my small amount of notoriety allowed me to sing in area churches. Today, many church services are as highly produced as a Super Bowl halftime show. Everything back then was a little bit more homegrown; there were no mega-sound systems, jumbotrons, or elaborate light setups. If you wanted a spotlight, a guy would stand next to the stage with a flashlight. You were lucky if the piano was tuned.

At my church in Marietta, I met a guy named Travis. He was a ginger with an athletic build and an analytical mind. He was hot, and he'd played college tennis and professional tennis, which gave him a muscular body. He wasn't flashy, but he was intellectual. I was chatty, but he was—shall we say—conversationally selective. A man of few words. But, like E. F. Hutton, when he spoke, people listened.

In other words, he wasn't my type. Historically, I swooned for the bad boys, but those guys didn't hold my interest any longer. I was quite content in being single, and even Travis, with his lopsided smile, wasn't going to change that.

One night after a gig, Travis and I chatted in a parking lot. That evening, as I droned on and on about Tina Turner, he decided in his heart that I was the woman he was going to marry. He believed God had great things for me and wanted to help me along that path.

Travis didn't hide his interest, but I didn't know how serious he was. He'd call and leave messages on my answering machine. (Yes, that's how long ago this was.). I'd listen to his messages asking me to call him back, then I'd go about my day.

"She wouldn't date you if you were the last man on earth," Amy once told Travis.

"You're sure about that?" he asked.

But my lack of interest didn't stop Travis and me from being friends. We hung out and talked endlessly about any and everything. Our love for music, our faith, and even my divorce. I felt comfortable with him. I could be myself around him. For one thing, I wasn't interested in dating him or any guy for that matter. Travis was more of a sounding board—a friend, yes, but a little like a counselor too. He would listen to me go on and on about how I wanted a career and how I never wanted to get married again. He would listen intently with a grin on his face like a Cheshire cat. It was like something was going on behind his smile. It wasn't tricky but I was sure it was mischievous.

Plus, the more I got to know Travis, the more I was impressed by him. A true individual, he didn't care about what other people thought about him. Whether someone liked him or not, he was who he was. He didn't put on airs, and I never saw him trying to be something he wasn't. Still, I didn't have any interest in a romantic relationship—but he didn't get the memo.

One night we went out to eat at a Mexican restaurant. When he walked me to my car, he leaned in and tried to kiss me.

"What are you doing?" I asked, putting up my hand. There were people all around, and some looked at us and snickered.

This move made me uncomfortable, and I almost *never* feel uncomfortable. I felt a flutter inside me, but it mainly made me mad. I felt out of control.

"Don't do that." I looked at him seriously, but he only smiled.

The man perplexed me, but I didn't have time to think about him. I had other things to focus on—mainly, my music. Like moths are drawn to a flame, aspiring musicians are drawn to Tennessee. Most aspiring musicians head to Nashville, but I couldn't get Memphis out of my head. So I asked the management company I worked for if they owned any apartment complexes in Memphis. As a manager of an apartment community, I could possibly find a new place to work within our apartment network and live rent free. My job gave me a lot of independence. I'm an educated risk-taker, not a dreamer. Neither am I an idiot, but I do move off my intuition. I let my gut be my guide.

"I feel like God is leading me to Memphis," I told Amy. This would affect her since we were roommates.

"Why?"

I threw my hands in the air. "I don't know! He didn't tell me all the details." And I'd asked Him. When I first contemplated leaving Atlanta, I started praying, but God was silent on everything except my need to get out of town. It was like He was saying, *I'm showing you nothing. I'm giving you nothing. But still, you gotta go.*

Have you ever felt the need to change, move, and step out of your comfort zone but have absolutely no idea why or if it will work out? Most people don't up and move for no clear reason—they move to change jobs, or they move to get closer to (or away from) family. Except for the Bible, you rarely hear stories of folks just packing up and leaving without a clear mission or on such a slim hope, with no idea what's coming next. But that was what that opportunity presented to me. It felt important, and I didn't want to miss it.

Amy sat down on my bed and plopped back on the pillow. I could tell by the look of incredulity on her face why most people don't take advantage of new, uncertain opportunities. What I felt led to do defied logic, because it looked like a backward move—quitting a good job and launching into the unknown.

"It doesn't make sense," Amy said while looking up at the ceiling.

"Maybe it's a whim or maybe it's just gas, but I feel the need to get out of town. Meet new people. Try something different. What do we have to lose?"

Looking back now, I realize part of me was running away from my mistakes, failures, and shame. But I was running right into the arms of a blind faith that would change everything. That's the essential ingredient for life. Faith picks up where hard work and logic leaves off. Faith is different from belief. Belief is based on something that probably could happen, whereas faith is not based on probability at all. Belief depends on proof, whereas faith does not.

Faith picks up where hard work and logic leaves off.

I had no idea what moving to Memphis would mean for me, but I wanted to find out.

"I feel like God is asking me, 'Do you trust Me? Do you have the faith to do what I say when I say it? Then just go ahead and step out without knowing all the details,'" I said.

I thought it would be fun if Amy joined me on the Memphis

adventure. It took me a few weeks to persuade her, but after I laid out the pros and cons, she relented. After we packed up all our belongings, we looked around the mostly empty apartment and noticed we forgot to pack our answering machine. "Grab that and stick it in this box," I said as I squished down the contents of the last box of odds and ends. "It'll fit."

Amy was just about to unplug it when she saw the red light was blinking. She pressed the button. Suddenly, the voice of Travis emanated from the machine, and then I heard the 1981 song by Stevie Nicks and Tom Petty filling the empty kitchen. It was called "Stop Draggin' My Heart Around," and the words came from the tiny speaker. Amy and I looked at each other and started laughing.

"Girl, he's got it bad," I said. Although Travis had great taste in music, his affection was not my concern. "Now, unplug that thing and let's go."

We drove to Memphis and unpacked our stuff in our new Tennessee place—Trinity Lakes Apartments. I tried to focus on getting a record deal but was distracted a couple of weeks later when Travis came to visit me.

We did all the things that tourists do, including the number one attraction in Memphis: Graceland. Going to Elvis Presley's home seemed like the perfect way to pass an afternoon. Built in 1972, Graceland represented the best (and possibly worst) of the decade. The plantation's white columns led to an all-white formal lounge featuring peacock-stained glass windows. There was the famous Jungle Room with its tiki bar, custom poodle wallpaper, a deep blue sectional couch, chrome arc lamps, a perfectly preserved 1970s kitchen, and shag carpet for miles.

As I was sitting on that shag carpet next to Travis, my whole life was changed by a simple motion.

Travis leaned over to whisper in my ear.

His nose grazed my neck, and I could hear his breath in my ear before he said a word. The words weren't important. I don't even remember them now. He might have made a snide comment about the gaudy room or maybe something about lunch. I can't remember one syllable of what he said. But what I do remember is that the slight smell of his aftershave caused every hair on my head to stand on end. I froze, not wanting to move and break the spell.

My hair has always been short and spiky, and I've never been able to toss it over my shoulder, like Cinderella. I've never had long, thick, shiny hair. But that day it was just long enough for Travis to reach up and, ever so gently, tuck my hair behind my ear.

Just as he began whispering, I gasped at this intimate and private moment meant for just us. As the guide droned on about the parties Elvis threw in his mansion, I wasn't thinking about the King of Rock and Roll. I was experiencing a moment, a realization that this man beside me had awakened something in me. This person I'd considered a friend for the past year. Nothing more. This man who'd left me messages in song, who could see me—*right through me*—more clearly than I could see myself. He'd known early on that he wanted to marry me, and I'd ignored his transparent adoration. I preferred men who were harder to get, challenges, even jerks. Travis was none of those things, but he knew what he wanted. He's nothing if not methodical.

You think methodical can't be appealing? Well, you weren't at Graceland that day.

Finally, Travis began to speak—and I had to lean in closer to hear him. No, that's not quite true. I leaned over to feel closer to him because I suddenly realized I wanted nothing more. Chill bumps arose on my arm, and I grabbed a handful of Graceland's shag carpet I was sitting on, digging my nails into the fiber. My whole body got warm. The moment was spiritual, musical, and historic.

It was also the moment I fell in love with Travis Gravel.

Who falls in love at Graceland? I did, baby.

Since becoming friends, I'd always been honest with Travis. He knew about my romantic mistakes. And my divorce wasn't a dealbreaker. A little of my shame was starting to melt away.

That night, Travis and I went dancing in a nightclub off iconic Beale Street, a neon-illuminated melting pot of the blues, gospel, jazz, and rock and roll. The band was playing the blues when Travis grabbed my hand.

"May I have this dance?" he said with a mock formality, then he looked out onto the packed dance floor.

"Is there enough room out there for us?" I asked.

"The more crowded, the better."

The music billowed around my head, and I felt as if I would float away. But I was tethered to Travis by the grip he had on my hand as we wove between pulsating bodies moving to the beat of the music. When we found a spot on the floor that could accommodate both of us—just barely—he put his hand on my hip, and we began to sway.

My face was so close to his collar I could smell the starch on his shirt, and he put his arms around me. For perhaps the first time, I noticed—no, I appreciated—how muscular he was. He was attractive, he was smart, and his hand was on my hip.

"You gonna show me some moves?" I laughed. But he didn't start dancing; he simply looked into my eyes, evaluating me. He pulled me closer to him, then suddenly twirled me like the ballerina in my childhood jewelry box. We laughed and carried on, like we were the only two people on the planet.

The next day, he was scheduled to drive back to Atlanta. But neither of us had mentioned the obvious chemistry that had sparked between us. Right before he walked out the door, I grabbed his arm.

"I have feelings for you," I declared boldly as I stood before Travis. I felt like Julia Roberts's character in the movie *Notting Hill* when she finally told Hugh Grant how she felt about him. Travis shifted from one foot to the other, and then I added, "You've been right about us all along."

He took my hands gently. I prepared myself for a long-awaited first kiss, the one that must've been my destiny ever since he'd tried to kiss me in that Georgia parking lot. But Travis didn't lean down and lay one on me. Instead, he squeezed my hand and let it drop to my side.

"I have to think about this." He smiled and turned to the door. "I'm not sure." Then he left.

My heart fell to the floor.

He drove back to Atlanta, and I expected to hear from him when he got home. But I didn't hear from him that day—or the next.

A few days later I told Amy, "He's never going to call."

"Well, he gave you plenty of chances already," she said. "You did ignore like fifty million messages."

"You're the one who told him I wouldn't date him if he was the last man on earth," I cried.

A week after that (what seemed like an eternity), the phone rang. I grabbed that receiver like it was a check from Ed McMahon.

"Hello?" I tried to sound casual.

"Kim, I've had time to pray, and I've come to the conclusion that . . ." It seemed like it was taking him forever to finish the sentence, so I sat down in a chair. "I do believe we should date," he said.

I didn't realize I was holding my breath, but apparently, I had been for the past several days. Nonetheless, I respected his game.

I was still filming my television show *Friends & Neighbors* in Atlanta, which meant I had to drive six hours in the morning to do a segment, then drive six hours back in the evening. The next time I drove to Atlanta for the show, Travis and I met at a Mexican restaurant for our first official date. After the meal, we walked to the car, where he kissed me—and I mean, *kissed* me.

Suddenly, I found myself in a long-distance relationship, right after I'd moved to Memphis. It wasn't super convenient, but I was happy that finally Travis and I were dating, and I was in a good place to focus on my career. But a record producer who had first shown interest in my music got sick and landed in the hospital for six months. I was trying to get a record deal, but I wasn't getting much traction.

Here's the crux of it. Back then, God asked me—in no uncertain terms—*Do you trust Me enough to do what I tell you to do when I tell you to do it?* He didn't move me to Memphis for an opportunity or to make connections. He moved me to Memphis to exercise my trust muscle. And I've been using it—with varying degrees of success—ever since.

You have to be willing to take God-sized risks. Be wild with it. It might not make sense in the moment, but God always makes sense in hindsight. Trust the hindsight. Remember what you've learned.

God's taken care of you, and He's gonna do it again.

I still didn't know God's exact path, but I can look back and connect some dots. Dating Travis probably would have never happened if I hadn't gone to Memphis and realized, in his absence, that I missed him. I thank God I chose to follow that still, small voice when He told me to go to Memphis. That's one of the values of writing all this down. I can get spiritual amnesia! Sometimes our routines are just ruts in disguise. Sometimes you have to jump without a safety net. Do something. Shake it up. Step out of your comfort zones.

Sometimes our routines are just ruts in disguise.

What has God been whispering to you? Have you been putting off taking your next step?

I discovered a lot about Travis while we were dating. Turns out, Travis was everything I never thought but always wanted: stable, steady, supportive, logical, analytical, and excellent with money (translation: "cheap as dirt"). I was the fence; he was the pole that holds the fence up. He's very strong (I guess he'd have to be, as a partner of mine, right?). He wasn't sensitive and was never offended. I fought, but he never did. When I lost my temper, he'd simply listen. Then, after a few moments of me fussing, he'd say, "Are you done?" He vexed me, but he was exactly what I needed. He was a huge catalyst for me overcoming my shame veiled as cheap confidence. He saw me. The real me.

Taking that risk to move to Memphis was a confidence builder. I no longer felt like damaged goods, and I felt like together Travis and I could do anything.

On New Year's Eve of 2000, when everyone was talking about Y2K, Travis came to visit me in Tennessee. He took me to see the Tom Hanks movie *Castaway* (which was partially shot in Memphis) and then to the Opryland Hotel in Nashville. This hotel is a modern marvel because it houses fifty thousand plants in its three enormous atriums. My mouth was hanging open as I looked at all the palm trees and banana trees on what seemed like every square inch of that hotel. Travis pulled me to a private corner with a little black bench and began professing his love. Suddenly, to my surprise, he got down on one knee and pulled out a ring.

It was a diamond ring, his mother's, who had died when he was a teenager. I knew that ring meant the world to Travis, and my heart felt like it was going to beat right out of my chest. Right there in that plant-filled atrium, he asked me to be his wife.

I couldn't say yes fast enough!

Maybe God knew that I needed to go to Graceland to figure out that I was in love with Travis. So I say to God, "Thank You. Thank You very much!"

Maybe God is asking you to do something that doesn't make any sense, just as He asked me to pick up and go—and leave my TV show, family, and Atlanta life behind. Maybe you're not totally sure of His plan or the faith that will be required of you in the future. Here's what I know. We don't leave enough room for the serendipity of life. How are we supposed to do that? Well, for me, it was following God and taking a chance and moving. My move to Memphis was when my more adventurous faith walk really began.

There's a great quote in J. R. R. Tolkien's *The Fellowship of the Ring* that reminds me of this moment. "It's a dangerous business, Frodo, going out of your door. . . . You step into the Road, and if you don't keep your feet, there is no telling where you might be swept off to."[3]

Well, I stepped out of my door in Georgia and onto the road and got swept right into the arms of the man God had for me.

When's the last time you stepped out of your comfort zone? When's the last time you felt a call in your spirit, and you dismissed it, denied it, or ran from it? When's the last time you took a risk on *you*?

It's time for you to step out in faith. Do the thing. What are you waiting for? Are you waiting for the perfect circumstances? Are you waiting for everything to fall into place? Are you waiting to get younger? To get thinner? Or probably more to the point, do you think you've made too many mistakes to even try? "If you wait for perfect conditions, you will never get anything done" (Ecclesiastes 11:4 TLB).

After my divorce, I was ashamed. No more. I now know my mistakes are a part of my story, and they make up the flavor of who I am.

This is true for you too. Don't despise any part of yourself. There's a message in your mess. Embrace your mistakes. Reframe your "big mistake" as just a stepping stone. You're not too far gone. Embrace all of you. I mean all. Not just the fun, Instagrammable parts of you. Every bit of what you've done is part of who you are and who you're called to be.

I'm on an upward trajectory, but I still do dumb stuff. It's not like you decide to live a life of faith and suddenly you no longer make mistakes. Girl, I've made a million mistakes since I started writing this book. But that only means I'll have more material for the next one.

Your life is spiraling upward too. Your mistakes are not dragging you down; they are giving you more juicy material for your story. That's the good stuff.

Travis saw the real me in all my mess and still pursued me over and over like I was the most valued prize. After a year of long distance dating, Travis and I tied the knot. Got hitched. Yep, I got married again. I often tell Travis he wore me down, but truthfully he wooed me down. God woos you, pursues you, and chooses you. If where you are is not where you want to be, it's not too late. What if all the unanswered, unexplained things that have happened in your life are really your calling pursuing you? Just make sure your heart is open to the whispers of what's in store for you. How? Here's some advice, from someone who's done a lot of things wrong.

> What if all the unanswered, unexplained things that have happened in your life are really your calling pursuing you? Don't edit your story.

Don't despise any part of yourself. Every bit of what you've done is part of who you are and who you're called to be.

Don't edit your story.
Don't despise any part of yourself.
You're not behind.
It's good to be you.
You are not an oddity.
You are beautiful.
Embrace all of you. God does.

Four

Never Put Yourself on Sale

Your playing small does not serve the world. Who are you not to be great?

—Nelson Mandela

"My boss is leaving. She's quitting." Amy placed her fork down on her plate. "I don't know who I'm gonna work for who will give me the same sort of flexibility that she and the top boss, Fred, did." Her brow was furrowed, and Amy wasn't eating her food. She believed this was the end of the road for her career trajectory. I could tell by the way she was slouching over her plate.

Have you ever struggled with your self-worth? Some of you may have already guessed that Amy, my roommate from the last chapter, is also the same Amy who shows up on my social media a great deal. My BFF. The one with the fiery red hair. But Amy wasn't always *Amy*, the empowered, strong woman.

One night, as Amy, Travis, and I ate dinner at the Mellow Mushroom, Amy was struggling to understand her worth. Just like many of you. Just like I do on a near-daily basis.

But battling for your self-worth does not mean you have to fundamentally change your personality. Amy was, and is still, an introvert. She's the yin to my yang. When I walk into a room, I go straight into the thick of things to see who I can hug. Amy cases the room in hesitation looking for someone interesting to chat with. She's smart, but back then, she didn't believe it. She's pretty, but she didn't see it. She's charismatic but didn't know it. But I wasn't worried.

This is our posture when we know we are capable, but our hope and imaginations fall short of our goals and desires. She was really just scared to death. "Chin up. This ain't the end." I had to remind her that she was sort of a big deal, because—like many of you—she played herself down.

Girl, I do this, too, so you're not alone.

As women, sometimes we dumb ourselves down. We play ourselves small and mistake opportunities for obstacles because of it. It's not that we're taking anything for granted, aren't grateful, or don't value what's been given to us. Our silent conviction that we aren't "all that much" seeps into our perspective on opportunities. If you're thinking, *How can something valuable happen to me?* I'm gonna stop you right there, just like I stopped Amy. That's not humility; that's self-loathing . . . an unhealthy mentality that's not doing you any favors.

"Don't worry about it," I said to Amy, waving my hands in the air. "Just get ready. Fred's gonna come to you and offer you your boss's job."

"Me?" She looked at Travis for backup. "This isn't some rinky-dink accounting job. It's an international software firm with global reach. I'm not qualified. I'm just the assistant."

"Mark my words: they're gonna offer you that job," I told Amy as I took a bite of pepperoni pizza with extra cheese. "And you better take it."

Sometimes Travis and Amy don't listen to me.

"You're insane. That's never gonna happen," Amy said before she and Travis brainstormed various other employment opportunities. However, a couple of days later, Amy announced, "Fred asked to meet with me tomorrow!"

"You mean, for that meeting where he's going to offer you your old boss's job?" I asked.

"No one offers someone like me a job like this." Amy rolled her eyes. "I don't have a master's degree."

Travis agreed.

"Let me ask you this," I pushed back. "Are you good at what you do?"

Amy looked like she'd never considered this question, but she nodded slowly.

"And could you do as good a job as your boss?" I asked.

"You don't understand the dynamics," she said. Travis also believed I was overreaching, but I knew in my gut I was right. I knew from what Amy had told me Fred was brilliant, and Fred knew Amy was smart. Amy just didn't recognize that she was smart or have the confidence to walk in it.

"If y'all don't shut up, I'm gonna leave," I said. People

always underestimate or fail to recognize what they're good at and try to fake what they want to be great at. You can get over others not believing in you, but you will *never* get over not believing in yourself. I knew this, but Amy and Travis obviously didn't. "Y'all are acting like I'm crazy or out of touch, but I'm right about this." They continued to ignore me and talk about other jobs Amy could scrounge around for and possibly get. I stopped trying to convince them.

> You can get over others not believing in you, but you will *never* get over not believing in yourself.

The next day, Amy went into the meeting and—guess what?—Fred said he had been monitoring Amy's work and had determined she could do the job.

"You're basically already doing her job anyway," he said. "So I want to offer you your old boss's position." Amy was floored and terrified. However, because she was in accounting, she knew approximately how much her boss had gotten paid for the same job. The amount Fred quoted for her salary was roughly $30,000 less than what her former boss had made.

"I'll think about this offer and get back to you tomorrow," she said. After work, she came straight over to Travis and my apartment and burst through the door.

"Girl, you won't believe this, he offered me the job," she said.

"What a surprise." I rolled my eyes. "Who would've ever guessed?"

She looked at me blankly.

"I called it, I told you!" I wanted at least some recognition that I'd been right all along.

Reluctantly, she nodded. Amy and Travis hate it when I'm right (which is not all the time but it is frequent, I must say). I might not be the sharpest tool in the shed but I could see this.

"Okay, but the salary is sort of . . . small." She explained how much he offered, compared to how much she knew her boss had made.

"You can't take the job for that money," I said. "That's too low. You're worth way more than that. You're gonna be just as good if not better than your boss that just left, so you need to ask for what you and the position are worth."

"I can't do it," she said. "I'm lucky to have been offered the position at all."

"Yes, you can," I said. "This is what you do." I stood up from the couch and pretended to be walking into the office. The kitchen table was the imaginary desk.

"Thank you, Fred, for this opportunity, but I'm not gonna do this job for such a little amount of money. I need to make $30,000 more." I looked over at Amy. "See? Easy. He'll have respect for you. He knows you; he's worked with you; he likes you. Believe me, he'll give you the money."

"I can't say that number out loud," she said. "I can't ask for that kind of money."

"Okay," I said slowly. I realized what I was dealing with now. I wasn't fighting Amy; I was fighting back against a culture in which women are afraid to establish their worth. Isn't it amazing how difficult it is for women to articulate what they want? What they need?

Most women, 60 percent, have "never negotiated with an employer over pay," and according to a report from the staffing firm Randstad, women "are much more likely than men to make a lateral move to improve their salary."[1] But I knew Amy's having a candid conversation with her new boss would be less work than looking for a new job that would also accommodate her after-hours singing schedule. If Amy had been a man, it's likely she wouldn't have thought twice about asking for more money.

So let's get this straight. I'm not talking about haggling, hustling, or trying to nickel and dime your employer. I'm talking about knowing your worth and being unafraid of stating it plainly. Research shows women are better able to negotiate higher salaries for other people than themselves,[2] which might have explained why I was so eager to convince Amy to know her worth. When I've had to negotiate on my own behalf, I've gotten butterflies too. Just being aware of this dynamic is enough to help you overcome your hesitance and state your worth.

"If you can't ask for it, then we'll do it another way," I said. "A power play."

"A power play?" Amy slouched in her chair. "Do you even know me?"

I did know her, and I knew her story. Amy's family had massive money issues. Not only was I pushing back against a culture that can undervalue women, but I was also up against the past money struggles that were stopping her from fighting for herself and saying what she needed and what she deserved. That's why I was adamant about Amy's not accepting this lowball offer. It felt important for her life beyond just a salary.

As women, we're conditioned to downplay our influence.

But think about Adam and Eve in the garden of Eden. Eve had power because she had influence on Adam. God Almighty had warned Adam, "Don't eat this fruit," but all it took was a few whispers from Eve to talk him into eating it. What kind of power of influence did this woman have?

Hopefully, we can use our powers of persuasion to better ends. Women inherently have power, but we often yield it differently than men. I don't walk into a meeting like some Girl Boss, but I do walk in knowing I have the power of influence. Too many women overvalue who they are trying to be and undervalue who they are.

Too many women overvalue who they're trying to be and undervalue who they are.

Is that probably you too? That's what Amy was doing.

I went back to the kitchen table and pulled out the chair.

"Tomorrow, when you go into his office, bring a pad of Post-it Notes and a pen. Then, in front of him, write down the salary you want on the top note, pull off the Post-it Note, turn it upside down, and slide it across the desk to him."

I demonstrated this with a slip of paper. I slid it across the table to her imaginary boss. "Then say, 'I've considered the position, but I feel more comfortable with this number.'"

Amy didn't move.

"You listening?" I asked. "Can you do that?"

She nodded, but she wasn't happy about it. She was angry. That's when I knew we were on the right track, that this was a thing she had to push through. But that requires growth. Discomfort. If you're comfortable, you might not be on the

If you're too comfortable, you might not be on the right path. So when something activates you or aggravates you, pay attention.

right path. So when something activates you or aggravates you, pay attention.

Amy didn't have the confidence to do that, at least not at that moment. That's the thing about confidence. She didn't need it as she was sitting in the comfort of our apartment; she needed it the next day. Sometimes when we consider doing something that requires courage, we don't feel like we'll be up for it. But when the time comes, your confidence will meet you in the moment. That's all you need.

"Take a seat first, and make sure you use his name," I said. "Don't leave the room without saying 'Fred' at least once."

"Who am I?" she asked me. "His elementary school teacher?"

"Listen, like Dale Carnegie said, 'A person's name is to that person the sweetest and most important sound in any language.'[3] Put yourself on his level. Yes, he's your former boss's boss. But saying his name makes him human. It individualizes him."

The next morning, Amy walked into the office and sat down at the table with Fred. She placed her pad of Post-it Notes and pen beside her.

"Thank you so much for this offer," she said, just as we had rehearsed. "But Fred, I would feel more comfortable with this number."

Then, she took the top off her pen, wrote down the salary she wanted, flipped over the note, and slid it across the desk.

Fred turned it over, read the number, and something akin to shock covered his face. He wasn't prepared for Amy's response. But quite quickly, the shock on his face morphed into a smile. He was impressed by her counteroffer, and he even seemed to respect it.

"Okay, let me talk this over, and I'll get back to you," Fred said. Amy, to her credit, thanked him and walked right out of the office. Sometimes you have to be willing to lose something to gain it.

> Sometimes you have to be willing to lose something to gain it.

The next day, Fred accepted her offer.

That was a big moment for Amy. Not only did it do wonders for her confidence, but the company was sold eventually to an even bigger company, and she made even more money. Not only did Amy get a new job, she got paid double what was offered! Now she looks back on that moment as a changing point in her life.

Some of you suffer from "imposter syndrome"—you believe you are not as competent as others perceive you to be. I get it. I frequently look at my life and think, *How on earth did I get where I am today?* But for those of you who suffer from imposter syndrome, like me, I have a simple and easy suggestion.

If you can't say what your strengths are, write them down. Go and get your own Post-it Notes and a big black Sharpie. Are you a good baker? Are you a good organizer? Are you good with numbers? Whatever it is, write it down now.

There is a story in the Bible where the prophet Habakkuk was instructed to "Write the vision; make it plain on tablets" (Habakkuk 2:2 ESV). I have to assume that's because sticky note technology hadn't been invented yet. Either way. Carve your worth into a stone, scrawl it on a tablet, or write it down

Don't put yourself on sale. Take yourself off clearance, baby. You're worth it.

somewhere. I like to use a Post-it Note, so try that. Take that Post-it Note and stick it to your bathroom mirror.

When you are brushing your teeth, focus on that Post-it Note and pray the right person will see the value you have to offer, and put yourself in positions to take advantage of your strengths. After you focus on the Post-it Note every day, who knows what could happen? You might get used to identifying with that unique strength that's all yours. Don't undersell how valuable you are. Don't be intimidated by it. Don't be cocky about it. Just move in it.

There's nothing more disheartening than seeing a powerful anointed person dumbing down their strengths. Don't do what Amy did initially! Trust me. You can come from a trailer park or Park Avenue. It doesn't matter. Don't put yourself on sale because you don't think you are worth in. Take yourself off clearance, baby. See yourself as a masterpiece, and don't slash the price. You are not less than. You are not last year's style. People respect people who know who they are and who won't accept less than they are worth.

Deep down you know who you are.

Start operating from that foundation of knowledge.

Titles and degrees don't make you confident. But if you are like me, the school of hard knocks has given you an education that could rival a degree from Harvard. (Let's be honest—even better!) You have real-world experience and common sense—a rare combination these days. If you are in the major leagues, don't accept minor league pay.

So never put yourself on sale. Are you hanging on the clearance rack? Take yourself out of the bargain bin and put yourself on display as the top of the line. Greatness costs what it costs, and you are worth every penny.

Don't let the world determine your value. Only then will you find out how much you're worth.

11 Ways to Be Authentic

1. Do your best with what you have.
2. Know your weaknesses but work on your strengths.
3. Spend time alone with yourself every day.
4. Know your values and *never* compromise them.
5. Remember we are all the same in different ways.

6. Stop trying to prove, just produce.
7. Don't barter your worth.
8. Don't let what you see talk you out of what you know.
9. See the success of others without seeing your failure.
10. Confidence is quiet; insecurity is loud.
11. No matter what anyone tells you, God always has a better word.

Five

Life Is Like a Jelly Doughnut

Failure is the condiment that gives success its flavor.

—Truman Capote

I always thought I was going to be a singer-songwriter. I hadn't made it in Nashville, but I couldn't let go of the dream . . . even if I pursued this dream in a small way. Amy and I formed a girls' group called Beloved, which traveled all over the country performing at women's conferences, churches, businesses—singing, talking, and connecting. The singing group was sort of an afterthought when I believed my dreams of singing had evaporated. This opened the world to me in ways that I wouldn't have been able to anticipate.

But that also meant travel and endless packing and unpacking. One day, I ran to the drugstore to buy nylons.

"What aisle are the hose on?" I rushed into the store and grabbed a little handbasket. I just needed to pick up a few things before packing for my next gig. I looked at the clock on the wall. I didn't have much time.

"Garden supplies, aisle 23." The kid was wearing a red shirt and had an eager face. He pointed to the back of the store.

"Not a garden hose." I stopped in front of the register. "Pantyhose."

His face reddened momentarily as he walked me to aisle 8 and quickly shuffled back to the register, leaving me with a wall of nylon options. I needed to look good for my upcoming church concert, so I needed a little tummy control. I'd put on a little weight after I got married. You know how, in college, they talk about gaining the "freshman fifteen"? After I got married, I gained weight, but it might've been closer to twenty.

Beloved's motto was "Real Music for Real Women." And I mean *real*. All of us were in our thirties. Things were starting to sag and hind ends were getting wider during a time when everyone else in the music industry was acting like they were auditioning for lingerie ads and having wardrobe malfunctions. I wasn't going to do that, but I was hoping that these control-top pantyhose could suck me in enough so my skirt wouldn't be too snug. "Real" had its limits.

I could keep my cellulite to myself.

Up until then, I would've just grabbed a package labeled B and headed out. But now, I needed to evaluate my options. I stood in the middle of the floor of aisle 8, holding several packages of pantyhose. I flipped one over to determine the size, which was based on height and weight, and my eyes glossed over. At the top of the chart were weights of the potential pantyhose wearer, starting at 90 pounds and going up. I placed my finger on the chart and slid to the right. And then to the right some more. And then a little more. Once I found my weight, I looked down the left-hand size of the chart and found my height. Your size was indicated where your weight and height intersected on the chart. The different sizes were color coded. A was pink (small), B was yellow (medium), but there was no C. The next size up, shaded green, was Q for "queen"—in some pantyhose manufacturer's attempt to make Cs sound regal, but we all know that means you have some junk in your trunk. It took a protractor to figure out what size you were on this Tetris-like chart. On that day, my fingers kept tracing down and down and down until I got to my size.

I had a sinking sensation.

Back before Google Maps was on every iPhone, you might accidentally veer off course on a road trip and finally get the folded-up, ratty map from the glove compartment to trace where you'd been and where you wound up. When you realized you weren't where you thought you should be, a certain dread came over you.

I felt that same feeling.

I looked at my fingers. They weren't where they should be. My fingers weren't on pink, yellow, or even green. They landed on purple. I was no longer a B. For that particular brand, I wasn't even a "queen."

I was a "queen plus."

"No," I said, putting the package back. "I will not have this."

"Do you need help finding anything?" The young cashier walked back to me, skittishly, like a cat, but the look in my eyes made him step around me and keep on going. The music on the intercom was easy-listening instrumental pop, but my heart was pounding. I put that package back on the rack and picked out a smaller pair, and said out loud to myself, "Get thee behind me Satan. I'm buying a B."

When I got home, I tossed the pantyhose in my suitcase and didn't think anything about them until I was at the Baptist church, trilling like Whitney, and looking good in my slacks, long pink trench coat, and bright top. I was singing my heart out, and the crowd really responded. Amy and I thought we'd be a little flashy and do an outfit change in the middle of the concert. So, while the pastor addressed the congregation, we slipped into a back room at the church, and I began to change into my too-tight skirt.

Are pantyhose even a thing now? For all you youngsters, they're like tights, but much worse. In fact, control-top pantyhose should be outlawed by the Geneva Convention as virtual torture devices; they cut into your belly and ride up (or down) your thighs. And the snagging. Look at them wrong, and they'll tear. I didn't want a part of any of that, so I carefully pulled the size B nylons out of the box and held them up. They looked like they *might* fit a Barbie doll.

"You ain't never going to get in them hose, girl," Amy said, as she changed clothes. It's amazing we're still friends.

"Wanna bet?"

I laid down flat on the floor and started pulling. Everything goes on better when you are lying down. When I stood up, they were so tight, I could feel my pulse. But I showed Amy. I squeezed into those suckers and looked good. They took me down a whole dress size. My skirt was so loose, I could hula hoop in it.

My confidence went to cockiness in one quick moment.

I pranced back out on the platform and was preparing to sing my heart out. The pastor was saying something very earnest and sincere, and it was up to us to bring it on home. For those of you who are not familiar with church, an offering plate is always passed.

My dad once told me, "Life is like a jelly doughnut: you never know what you get until you squeeze it." And boy, did the squeeze happen to me. The pantyhose were squeezing me to within an inch of my life. I stepped up and I started singing while people dropped coins into the wooden plates. But as I was singing, I felt something snap.

What was that? It was sudden and unexpected, so—in my shock—I looked down at my legs. My size B control-top reinforced-toe pantyhose looked like fishnet stockings in an instant. This was no snag. This run was like a dam had been released, and parts of me had spilled out right there on a platform in front of a full house. It wasn't a run that you could just put some clear nail polish on to stop it.

My mom would say, "Kim, put a little clear nail polish on that run. You can wear those pantyhose two more Sundays." Or if you were like me, you would use red or pink nail polish 'cause that was all you had. My legs each Sunday would look like I had the chicken pox.

I gasped as I saw the run shoot down my leg, my fat bulging out. It had been so tight that I could feel my cellulite had a pulse. I felt relief as the blood started circulating again. To my surprise, I stopped singing mid-song. I could tell the people in the first pews had a front-row seat to this explosion, because they were sitting there stone-faced watching what might happen next . . . like bystanders at a traffic accident trying to determine how bad it was going to get.

"Cut the track." I waved at the soundman. I couldn't finish my song. "Stop, stop, stop." Nothing quiets a church crowd more than when something unexpected happens. The audience could see what was going on. You could've heard a pin drop, or—as the case may be—a nylon thread giving up its valiant effort of keeping me in. On the front row sat a man wearing a short-sleeve button-up white shirt with a horseshoe of hair around his head. His mouth was slightly open in embarrassment on my behalf.

I had a decision to make.

Would I hide behind the piano and just try to get through the song?

Would I run off the stage in shame?

Would this be the end of my singing career?

The nylon explosion was a moment of weakness that could have resulted in my alienation from others. Nothing like this had happened to me before. But at that moment, I decided to embrace it. I went with it. I decided not to take myself so seriously. That night, I found my funny.

I'd wanted to be my old 115-pound, size-B self. Honey, that's not who I was anymore. I was in denial about so many things. And I was being squeezed—literally and figuratively—and the funny that was always on the inside came pulsating out.

Do you ever feel this way? As we age, change, and move forward in life, we aren't who we once were. Sometimes, women feel melancholy as we age, because we get stuck on the image of our former selves. But the past is over. The good news is that something better, freer, and even more authentic is on the horizon. The squeeze. And through life's pressures we are honed. Coal becomes a diamond under pressure. Standing on that stage in those too-tight hose was pressure for sure!

When we were in our mothers' wombs, God fashioned us for greatness. A lot of times the squeeze and pressure of life, the mistakes, the things that happen to us, helps us to remember that. It might look different on the outside, but the best part of the jelly doughnut is the jelly. God allows painful things to happen so that we can rediscover that yummiest, most authentic part of ourselves that comes out when that pressure is applied.

So think about those times when the pressure was on in your life. What did you learn from it? How did you grow from it? What's your pantyhose story? Look in that mirror again, the one we started with at the beginning of this book. What do you see? What's on the inside of you?

I was about to discover what was inside of me. I could've walked away *in* shame, but I didn't walk away at all. My feet didn't move—even though my fat was jiggling—but I walked away *from* shame. I made eye contact with that man in the front row, the man whose eyes were full of shock, compassion, and embarrassment. I spoke directly to him.

"Sir, you need to be very afraid." I leaned down and spoke into the microphone. His eyes got wide. "Because my pantyhose are getting ready to give way, and you're right in the line of fire."

When that man dutifully got up and rushed to the back row, the entire congregation erupted into laughter. They just lost it. It was the most transcendent moment. Nobody cared that I'd just botched my song. I was no longer a wannabe Whitney. That was over. I was just me, standing there as my queen-sized self, laughing along with an audience full of people who were thankful that finally something hilarious had happened in church that night.

And it was a moment of pure, unadulterated joy.

I'm not sure I ever felt as liberated, as free, or as exuberant. It changed my whole life. Because right there on the stage—my cellulite pulsing and the audience laughing—I realized what I was made to do. I wasn't created to strut my stuff, to impress people, or even to sing. I never thought of myself as comedic, but everyone laughed. Though my calling isn't to make people laugh or tell jokes on stage, I realized in that moment that's sometimes a part of it.

My calling was to connect with people. Dad told me this long ago: "Don't just sing; always talk." I didn't understand that at the time, but all of that came rushing back to me on that stage. I was no longer a singer performing for the audience. I was connected to them in a powerful way that elevated all of us. Realizing what I was supernaturally gifted to do was a feeling like none other.

There's nothing like it.

Amy probably feels that way when she's working and organizing things. A basketball player might experience it when he dunks the ball. In the movie *Chariots of Fire*, Olympic athlete Eric Liddell said, "I believe God made me for a purpose, but he also made me fast. And when I run I feel His pleasure."[1]

That's what I felt on that stage: God's pleasure. When you walk in your calling, you bring so much joy to yourself and others. And to be honest, my pantyhose have been exploding ever since. From that moment on, I didn't take myself so seriously, and I didn't collect my confidence from something like a loose skirt or my appearance—stuff that can change (I now realized) in an instant.

When you walk in your calling, you bring so much joy to yourself and others.

So, what is the squeeze for you?

If we squeeze you, what's going to come out? I'm not talking about your junk—your hurts and pains and the people who have done you wrong or what you've done wrong. I'm talking about the good part. The yummy part, just like the middle of the jelly doughnut.

If you can't answer that question, maybe you need to squeeze a little harder. Life is hard, but God is good. He uses every ounce of who we are.

After the audience's laughter died down and the collection plates had been passed, the church received more money from that offering than ever before. God's economy is different than yours. In the television show *Stranger Things*, the Upside Down is an alternate dimension to what we see in the human world. But that ain't got nothing on God. In God's upside-down kingdom, weakness is strength, failures are successes, and embarrassment is power.

Explode into that power the next time you feel the squeeze . . . and just sit back and see what God will do with the best parts of you that burst forth.

Six

I'm Not a Fat Girl

When the heart is right, the mind and the body will follow.

—Coretta Scott King

"Isn't he an angel?" The older lady in the grocery store line peeked at my baby son, Beau, as he slept in the car seat, nestled in the front of the cart. I'd been at the store for an hour, and he'd screamed the first fifty minutes. I wasn't sure how many of the items on my list I'd actually managed to get, but I spotted a box of Grape-Nuts cereal in the cart, and no one in our family even ate those.

I hadn't washed my hair. I didn't have the two-day dirty hair that gives you volume and thickness. I had five-day dirty hair that makes people take a step back. As I stood there next to the rack of *Cosmopolitan* magazines proclaiming, "How to Get the Look Guys Crave," I realized my shirt was stained with milk. From last week.

The lady looked at Beau again and then gave me a knowing smile. "This is the best time of life, and it doesn't last long, so enjoy it."

In my mind, I said, *Lady, are you kidding me? I'm exhausted and have no clue what I'm doing.* But I'm a southerner, so I simply smiled.

These were the best days? Was this all I had to look forward to?

I felt like my life was going to be like this forever. My whole life would be raising my kids, and I felt like everyone kept assuring me that this was enough. But it wasn't enough. I was content, but I wasn't satisfied.

The cash registers beeped in the grocery store, a monotonous symphony of boring, everyday life.

Beep. Beep. Beep.

"Enjoy this precious time with your baby. He is a gift." The lady's small-talk stirred up feelings of anger in me, and I wasn't sure why. She started putting her frozen meals on the conveyor belt. "It goes by so fast you won't believe it."

Beep. Beep. Beep.

All I needed to do was get through this checkout line without me or Beau having some sort of breakdown. It seemed that wherever I went, women told me I was supposed to have warm, fuzzy feelings about this time of life. But I didn't. And then I felt guilty about not feeling the way I was supposed to feel, so maternal doubt crept in.

The baby got distracted by the fluorescent store lights,

and the lady turned away from me. I breathed a sigh of relief. I like to talk to strangers as much as anybody—okay, more!—but she was acting as if motherhood was some sort of magic elixir, and if it was, that's not what I was experiencing.

Travis and I didn't jump into having babies. We'd been married six years by the time we started having children. We enjoyed our lives, routines, late-night television binging, sleeping in, and our careers. Now, don't get me wrong. When I was sitting at church a few pews behind a gurgling cutie, I always waved and blew kisses during the prayers. But back then, babies were for other people—couples ready to settle down and give up lingering brunches over the newspaper and coffee. I knew motherhood alters your life, can pause your personal dreams, and most definitely changes your priorities. Motherhood was a huge responsibility. I knew it would be an all-encompassing, full-time job, if I did it the way I wanted to. To be honest, I was scared to death. I know I was blessed not to struggle with infertility or marital problems (at least with *this* marriage). But, girl, we enjoyed those six years without kids.

In the very first episode of my TV show *Friends & Neighbors*, I had looked directly at the camera and said, "I need a man." The entire crew giggled. But I traveled across the nation to speak at women's conferences about all the things that women deal with. I'd wanted certain things, and I got them all. So why was I feeling so empty? It seemed the whole world considered motherhood the best thing that could happen to a woman, and I was supposed to ignore all the difficulties and sink into the syrupy sweetness of the experience.

That was not happening.

Motherhood was a grind. It was the same, day in and day out.

When you are a kid, you have such a limited perspective that you think you are the main character in the world's drama. That's natural. But as you grow, you learn—pretty fast—that everything doesn't revolve around you. Motherhood takes you to a different level of realization. Not only are you not the main star in the world, but you're also not even the main star in your own house. Suddenly, I was taking second place in my own life.

This was exactly what I was fearful of. I was not a dreamy person who believed the fairy tale of cute, quiet babies and a picket fence. I come from a family of raw realists. My own mom waited six years to have me, and then she waited another six to have my sister because she didn't know if she wanted another child.

My resistance to motherhood had nothing to do with a fear I couldn't love a child. It had everything to do with losing a little bit of who I was. But nothing can truly prepare you for motherhood.

Once I became a mother, I'd get out of bed, but I wouldn't want to. I'd bathe, but not as regularly. I wore sweatpants and oversized shirts to camouflage my ever-expanding waistline. It was expanding because I couldn't lose the baby weight I'd gained. I would look in the mirror and feel myself getting bigger.

Back in 2007 it wasn't the "You go, girl, rock it just the way you are" era. Beauty had a narrow definition, and I wasn't narrow enough to fit into it. I was depressed. My professional life singing and performing was slowing down. I feared "domestic bliss" was all I had to look forward to.

But it wasn't very blissful.

Some might call that ungrateful; some would say I was selfish. But pain is pain, girl. Sometimes people paint motherhood with an impressionist brush. Swaths of emotional language that miss the harder-edged details. I'm just being transparent about my experience.

I used to put on makeup and wear high heels, inspiring women at conferences. I now found myself at home with a crying child. I used to have television cameras pointed at me. Now the only thing pointed at me was a projectile-vomiting baby. For me, motherhood was mind-numbing. I'm a social person, but I didn't have anyone to talk to. When Travis came home from work, it was like we were playing pass the hot potato. The second he walked in the door, I basically threw Beau to him like Tom Brady throws a touchdown pass—retired or not. Then I'd head out the door to go to Target just to have some peace. Those strolls down the home décor and rug aisle were a little bit of heaven on earth.

I ate while I watched bad reality TV. It was so bad. It was good. I'd eat popcorn and Almond Joy candy bars—a craving from pregnancy that never let go—while watching *Clean House* on the Style Network, living vicariously through Niecy Nash and Trish Suhr. I'd eat ice cream while watching *Jon & Kate Plus 8*. I used to watch that woman struggling with her kids and say aloud to the screen, "Kate! I know, girl, call me!" I even got her long-in-the-front and spiky-in-the-back haircut. I was also obsessed with Ridge Forrester on *The Bold and the*

Beautiful—the old Ridge with the chiseled jaw, not the new Ridge. For a little inspiration, I also watched the preacher T. D. Jakes on TV. Anything to get me away from *Peppa Pig* and *Backyardigans.*

Going to visit my parents gave me a little reprieve. That week, I decided to drive to my parents' house. They lived about an hour away, and the baby fell asleep in the car. Pure freedom. I turned on the radio, sang, and tried to remember when life was easier and—to be honest—happier.

"I don't know what you're so upset about," Mom told me when I told her about my grocery store encounter the previous day. She and Dad were retired and comfortable. They slept anytime they wanted. I sat and watched as Mom fed Beau gunky baby food that looked like paste. She looked me in the eye and said, "It *is* the best time of life; you just don't know it yet."

This made me so mad. But why did this statement draw so much anger?

It was bad enough that strangers everywhere I went tried to tell me this, forcing me to grit my teeth that I might not have had time to brush. Now my own mother?

"I love Beau, but I miss all the stuff I used to do." I sank into the chair, thankful someone else was feeding Beau. He spit out the food, and it dribbled down his chin.

High heels, makeup, microphones, audiences, camera time, speeches . . . all replaced by sippy cups, bottles, bibs, cribs, and baby checkups. It was clear I was grieving my previous life.

"Why do you even want to be on television anyway?" Mom asked. She wiped away the food on Beau's face and tried again. "Open wide!"

"I've had a taste of it already, Mom," I said, reminding her of my ten-year stint on my talk show *Friends & Neighbors.* "Why would God bring me a TV show out of the blue and have me do it for ten years if domesticity is my fate?"

I felt like I was going backwards, drying up, but somehow getting bigger. (Ever feel like you are going backwards?) I was feeling less confident about myself. (Ever lose your confidence?) I'm a hard worker, someone who likes to add value. Though I was thankful to Jesus for my son, I had two simultaneous feelings: I absolutely loved my son, and I didn't want to bury my dreams.

My dreams felt as if they were dying under the heavy weight of motherhood. I'd felt so alive when I sang with the group Beloved. Amy and I had been successful. We made many albums, wrote many songs, and we traveled the country singing and ministering.

But now I had relabeled myself.

Not "mom." Worse. I was "just a mom."

I know I'm not alone. I hear it all the time. "Kim, I can't go back to college and finish my degree. I can't start that business. I can't pursue my dreams . . . I'm just a mom."

Motherhood is the most confusing, discouraging, loving, amazing time of a woman's life. Mostly, it's discombobulating, because your life is no longer your own. But you're taking all kinds of cues from the culture about how you are supposed to feel. And, honey, you are supposed to be happy. Appreciative. Satisfied. We live in a culture in which we are told we can have it all and do it all.

Well, I couldn't.

How are you supposed to have it all when you can't even bathe regularly?

Beau had fallen asleep, and Mom was watching him, so I went down to the basement to hang out with my dad.

"It's like a furnace down here," I said as I plopped down on their brown pleather couch. My dad's so cheap he doesn't use the air conditioner unless the walls are melting. He's as tight as a clothesline. A box fan sat on the floor whirring, but it just moved hot air from one place to the other. There was hardly any circulation.

"People have lived without air conditioning for most of human history," he said. "I think you can survive the afternoon."

He was just being my dad, but I began to cry. It wasn't that I'd had a particularly bad week; it was that I had a normal week—just like the one before, and it would be just like the one after. Those weeks were suffocating me.

"What's wrong with you?" he asked.

"It's not the heat." I shifted around on the couch. The sweat had caused my legs to stick to the pleather. "It's everything. I'm tired. My clothes don't fit; I'm spilling out of them."

My dad placed his hand on my shoulder, and I recoiled. I didn't want anyone to touch me. I wanted to be invisible, but being invisible made me angry. I really didn't know what was wrong with me. I didn't feel seen or heard. At the same time, I didn't want to be seen or heard. I was numb. I put my head in my hands. I felt like I couldn't shake my spirit of dread, like I was trying to run in knee-deep water.

"My dreams have passed me by." By now, I was sobbing. I was stuck. In life and on that sofa. If I stood up, with all that sweat, the couch would've ripped the flesh right off me. I was completely drenched. "I'm so fat. Out of shape. Everything's over."

"Why are you spouting off about your entire life being over, based on this one moment in time?"

I let my dad's question hang in the air. I listened to the dull monotony of the whirring fan. For a few moments, Dad didn't say another word. He was processing what I'd told him. Then, in that hot, uncomfortable basement—in my suffocating, uncomfortable life—my dad said words I'll never forget.

"Kim, you're not a fat girl. You're just living like one."

The world stopped.

With that one sentence everything came into focus. How I looked at everything changed; my circumstances, my body, my dreams, my calling came alive in an instant. My eyes were opened. Listen, my friend, you're not a broke girl, or an old girl, or a fat girl. The circumstances you are in are not who you are. We often confuse our "do" with our "who." Wherever you find yourself in your life right now, it's temporary. It's a moment in time. You're in it to learn, to grow, and to collect the confidence you need for the next level of your life. Circumstances, no matter how hard, good, or mundane—are there to propel us to whatever we are meant to be. Where you are right now is simply the starting place on the way to wherever you are meant to be.

So be careful when you begin a sentence with "I am." That's what my dad always told me.

"You're declaring *I am*, like it was the gospel truth," he would tell me. "But that's not who *you are*."

Girl, when you say I am fat, I am broke, I am sick, or I am (fill in the blank), you're lying to yourself. It's not true. The

Where you are right now is simply the starting place on the way to wherever you are meant to be.

truth is you are redeemed, you are whole, you are worthy, you are smart, and you are beautiful.

Right now, replace your "I am" with who you really are. Let's do it together, because I am who He says I am, thank you. (That's Bible, y'all! Look it up, boo.)

I am ______________________________________.

I am ______________________________________.

I am ______________________________________.

What did you answer? If you didn't say, "I am fearfully and wonderfully made" (Psalm 139:14), you did it wrong. Quit spouting off at the mouth, saying negative things, and digging the ditch deeper like I did. Be careful about what follows your "I am" statements. Change your "I am" to reflect who God created you to be.

That's what happened when my dad told me, "You're not a fat girl; you're just living like one." His words cut through the hair to get to the ham. For those of you who didn't grow up on a farm, a hog has thick, coarse hair. And it takes a lot to get to the meat. But Dad had cut right to it.

His words struck me. I looked up at him. He knew that what I was grappling with (or complaining about) was not about no longer fitting in my pre-pregnancy jeans.

"Kim, you're not done with your dreams. You're doing something else right now," Dad said. "And it's tough. Right now, you have another purpose in life—raising a boy."

I pondered his words for the rest of the night, and I'm still pondering them now and will continue to do so the rest of my life. Dad was saying, you're not your current circumstance. You're not your current habits. You're not your current situation. That's what the women were telling me too, right?

Motherhood was temporary? I needed to quit putting permanent labels on myself because of a temporary situation.

My incorrect perspective about motherhood had prohibited me from enjoying the moment or hoping for the future. I was grieving what I thought I'd lost without seeing the joy that was before me. Yeah, I needed to lose weight and get healthier. I would've felt better about myself, but that wasn't gonna fix me on the inside either. I was identifying with and making decisions out of a temporary, hard place. What I was looking at and how I was looking at it—both were skewed.

> You're not your current circumstance. You're not your current habits. You're not your current situation.

I will always value that sweat-drenched hour in that sweltering basement. You might be in your own "basement of life" now too. Don't miss the moment. Rarely do you really ponder your life when you are on a mountaintop. You reevaluate only when your life is so bad it jolts you into contemplation. God was using my motherhood experience to grow me up, to mature me, to get me into a place of readiness for a wonderful future that seemed elusive, and I just couldn't visualize it.

If you're frustrated and in your own "basement of life," know this and remember. Whatever you are doing right now is not who you are. I was identifying as an exhausted new mom with a few pounds to lose, but that's not who I was. Those are the circumstances I was living in, and those circumstances changed as rapidly as my waistline. I was placing all my self-worth on that one image of myself as a mom in a particular moment in time.

I realized that the only way I was gonna find true confidence was by placing my identity in something that never shifts, that never changes, and is always real. I was seeing it all wrong. The more I reaffirmed who God created me to be and who I really am, the more my behavior began to reflect true confidence. That day in that basement, my dad truly set me free.

I don't know if Dad intended to do that, but he did.

My melancholy was caused by a host of factors. Yes, I was grieving the loss of my career—my singing career. But I was also afraid. I knew what kind of work it would take to be a good parent—especially for an all-in person like me—and quite frankly, the responsibility terrified me. I thought I was gonna have to give up who I was to be what Beau needed.

But I was wrong. I didn't have to give that up, and God was changing me into more of who I truly was. Over time, the more I reminded myself that God had made me fearfully and wonderfully and that my identity was found in who God said I was—not in who others said that I was or what I was experiencing temporarily—my confidence started to grow and grow.

I had been operating from the "less than" of what I'd lost when I became a mother and not from the "more than" of what I had gained. Why do we fear loss when we have everything to gain? Why do we identify with loss? Always remember your gains are not always obvious in the moment. They're always more obvious in retrospect.

Why do we fear loss when we have everything to gain?

Whether you're struggling with motherhood or something else in your life, ask yourself these questions: How have you given up on yourself? What dreams have you stopped pursuing? As you contemplate the answers, don't beat yourself up. God has more for you, girl. You might not be able to see what He has in store for you. I get it. I was once right where you are. Now that I'm on the other side I know that more is coming for you. Just believe.

The "not okay" is temporary and the "okay" (beyond okay!) is promised. It's coming. Don't look around and feel overwhelmed, thinking your current situation is permanent. It, like your life, is but a breath. A vapor.

Mamas, you don't have to give up who you are when you have kids. There's no better gift to give to your children than allowing them to see you operating in the giftings God gave you. But life might feel like death for a while because you are in a mysterious, God-ordained process that will allow you to emerge victorious at the right time.

Guess what? That little old lady at the grocery store was right.

I miss those times with my baby. I would give anything to be awakened in the middle of the night by Beau's cries. Okay, maybe not the ear-deafening shrieks but definitely the easy-to-soothe whimpers that came from the crib. I've forgotten the times of exhaustion but miss the times of tender intimacy. I wish I could listen to his sweet gurgles as he drinks milk, smell the powder in his wispy hair, and squeeze his fat little fingers. I wish I could go to him in the morning, sweep him into my arms, and hear his laughter. I even wish I could snuggle on the couch with him as he sat in my lap and we watched *Peppa Pig*.

Motherhood turned out to be one of those "everything I never thought I always wanted" things. It was torture and torment. For a time, I felt like I was mourning. I was dying to my goals and dreams and learning to put others first. I couldn't stand it and then I loved it and then I hated it and then I loved it again. Motherhood is work, but I wouldn't trade it for anything.

Now I don't remember the exhaustion of early motherhood. I remember the inexplicable, tired, quiet joy of it.

These days when I see a woman struggling with a child, her hair mussed and the baby soiled, I might walk up to her and admire the baby. But do you know what I say to her?

"You've got a tough job, mama."

But in my mind, the words that older lady in the grocery store spoke to me come to mind and I add something I'd never say aloud.

Enjoy it while it lasts. It's truly the most beautiful time of life.

Down-Home Words of Wisdom from Mom and Dad

KIM GRAVEL

1. The deeper the roots, the sweeter the fruit.
2. Stop proving it, just produce it: A tomato plant doesn't have to prove it is a tomato plant.
3. You can't soar with the eagles if you scratch around with a bunch of turkeys.
4. If no one encourages you, encourage yourself.
5. Your losses are the fertilizer that nourish your success.

6. Stop being concerned about what others *might* think of you and remember this: they aren't thinking about you at all.
7. Every experience is a teacher. So go out and get your PhD.
8. Fighting change is like a toddler having a temper tantrum.
9. You can't help it if a bird lands on your head, but you can prevent it from staying and making a nest.
10. In the jungle of life, you have to use a machete and carve your own path.

Seven

The Mess Is the Message

"Call to me and I will answer you, and will tell you great and hidden things that you have not known."

—Jeremiah 33:3 ESV

A lady put her hands on my waist, and I took off through the Hilton ballroom as the hit song "Gangnam Style" blasted over the speakers. I was at the head of the conga line, and I watched as more than three hundred women followed my lead.

I felt strong. Empowered. I love being with other strong women, and I like to think the conferences Amy and I put on were a bit different than other women's conferences across America. In our annual Beloved conference, we cut loose and let our hair down. We sang, jumped on tables, and poured it all out like when we were teenagers at a Bon Jovi concert.

I was thinking of how much fun I had at the conference when I went in for a routine maternity checkup the next day. All the fun and games came to an abrupt halt while I sat in the doctor's office.

"I'm going to have to deliver the baby now; you need to check into the hospital," my doctor said to me as he looked at the results of my ultrasound.

"What?" I already had Beau, but at thirty-eight years old, I was pregnant again. I was not prepared for this moment, because the baby wasn't due for another eight weeks. How could I go from dancing and shaking my groove thing at the conference the previous night to delivering a baby that day?

The answer was simple. Because I had gestational diabetes and my blood pressure was rising, the doctor believed it was the right time for the baby to be born.

"He'll be premature, but he'll be fine," the doctor said.

After I was admitted to the hospital, I sat up in the bed and began to prepare myself emotionally.

"We're going to give you medicine to soften the cervix to allow easier dilation and get the contractions going." The doctor smiled encouragingly.

"Now?"

"No, not now. You're going to be here for a while," he said. "So just get comfortable and hang out. The baby won't come until probably—" He consulted his watch and sighed a little too heavily. He seemed annoyed at having to stay up late. "Definitely past midnight. Maybe three o'clock in the morning, if we're lucky."

It was only nine thirty in the morning, so we had time!

I started to feel badly that the doctor was having to work late, but dang, I was the one who'd be in labor overnight. He left, and I was sent to the labor and delivery floor. I didn't have my emergency suitcase with me because I thought I was just going for a regular checkup. I called Travis and my parents to tell them what was happening.

"Don't rush up here, though," I said. Honestly, I was enjoying having a moment alone. I was always living by the clock, with so many people demanding my attention. It probably says a lot that I was looking forward to being alone, because in my life at the time, labor and delivery was *less* stressful than normal life as a mom. "They aren't inducing yet, but it should all start happening late tonight."

A student nurse put in an IV to give me fluids and to later administer the medication to induce labor. I planned on settling into the hospital bed and pulling the white sheets up to my chin to rest for the long process ahead. I had my movie set up on my laptop—*Pride and Prejudice*—and was already looking forward to Mr. Darcy's famous lines: "You have bewitched me, body and soul, and I love, I love, I love you."[1]

I didn't even make it to the opening scenes. A few minutes after the nurse left, I felt a pain unlike anything I'd ever felt before. My hand clenched the rail of the bed. I couldn't breathe; I couldn't move. It was all I could do to press the button to alert the nurse. A few moments later, she came in, a cheery expression on her face.

"I'm dying," I gasped.

I don't remember what she said. I'm not even sure I could hear what she said. But I felt her general vibe was a little frosty.

She probably just expected women in labor to be in pain, but I was not in labor. They had not induced me, and the doctor had told me the baby wouldn't come anytime soon.

The nurse smiled politely and left me alone in the room. *Why had I told Travis and my parents not to hurry?* The pain surged through my body like a wave, and I thought I was going to die—right there, alone, in a hospital gown. I felt like I was going a little bit crazy. I'd told the nurse that I felt like I was dying. Why didn't she help me? Why didn't she get what I was saying?

Slowly, I made my way into the bathroom and sat on the toilet, hoping a change in position would help alleviate the sharpness of the stabbing pain. It didn't. A few moments later, the nurse came back to check on me.

"Everything okay?" she said.

"I'm dying," was all I could say. I know it sounds dramatic, but the pain was dramatic. I didn't have the emotional energy to explain. You'd think this would get her attention, to make her investigate. But she only smiled, and said, "Stay calm." Those words had the opposite effect on me. There's nothing more devastating than when people don't believe what you're telling them, ignoring your plainly stated need. But I couldn't say anything else. I was trying to convey, *I'm hurt. Something isn't right. Please help me.*

Again, the nurse didn't get it. I'd already given birth once, so it's not like I was shocked that bringing a baby into the world hurts. What I was experiencing now was different.

That student nurse left, and I sat there for what seemed like twenty minutes and stared at the floor of the bathroom. I tried to focus on the lines, the crisp squares of the tiles, but they seemed to undulate—like how blazing summer heat makes a Georgia road seem hazy and alive. I felt myself going in and out of mental clarity. Things were fuzzy. I was hot.

In an instant, I looked down and blood was everywhere. Blood was on the toilet, all over my gown, and—*what was happening? How did it get on the wall?*

I'd thought something was seriously wrong, but now I knew. I tried to stand, but I fell to the floor.

I was on my knees on that cold floor, my pregnant belly hanging beneath me. My hands were covered in blood. In less dire circumstances, I might've felt nauseated at the sight of so much blood, but I wasn't well enough to be sickened by it. I just knew I was dying, and I wasn't able to feel queasy.

I felt like a fever was ravishing my body. I was so hot I couldn't catch my breath. At first, I tried to figure out how to fight what seemed inevitable. *Should I crawl out to the hallway and scream? Should I cry out?* This is not a story of me overcoming my fear by using positive thoughts. No, I didn't have the ability to tell myself things were better than they were.

I was terrified.

But I was out of options. In movies, people who are about to die become super resourceful—they make tourniquets out of dental floss and dismantle a bomb with a bobby pin. I had none of that ingenuity. I had done everything I knew to do. I'd asked for help several times, and now I felt hot and confused. I knew very little, but I knew this was the end for me.

Everything up until this point had been happening so fast. But then, I let go of my scrambling to control what was happening, and everything slowed down. It was sort of like watching a video in slow motion, but it was different than that.

It was like I was being taken out of time itself, into a different realm governed by different laws of physics.

I was sitting there with just me, God, and the baby inside me. I had no doctor, no nurse, no pill, no family, no backup plan. God was all I had. All my striving ceased, and I was still. Everything was still. Quiet. Calm. Slow.

I didn't say this aloud, but I had a conversation with God. In my head, I told God this: *Lord, it's on You. This is it. I'm dying. If You see fit to let my baby live, please do. But this is on You. I'm out. I'm done. I ain't got nothing. I've got no strength. I got no power. I got nothing.*

And when I said this, the fear lifted, like the fog dissipates when the sun rises. There was something strangely comforting about not fighting the fear and accepting it. I felt my humanness fully at the same time I felt God fully.

Within that humanness, there was relief. Within that relief, there was confidence.

I didn't have to show anyone I was powerful. I didn't have to show anyone I was perfect. I didn't have any responsibility. I didn't have to do the right thing; I didn't have to say the right thing. I could just sink into what was happening to me and yield to God's control over my next breath, which—for the first time in my life—wasn't guaranteed. My fear left and was replaced by a deep, calm, penetrating peace.

Then, slowly, I looked up and saw a light.

It was more than light, actually. It's so hard to describe since words don't quite capture it. It wasn't like any normal light.

Imagine being in a dark cave for a while, and then someone finally turns on a flashlight. You can understand that seeing that light in darkness also might accompany an experience of hope and relief. Love and warmth. I was washed in something sort of like that. It went all over me. It went through me. I don't know what else to call it. The closest thing I can compare it to is light, so I guess that will have to do.

In that light was God. I saw His presence but not with my eyes. I felt His presence. The pain, which had been so agonizing it felt like a weight on me, just vanished. Gone. Like it was nothing. My eyelids grew heavy, and I felt loving arms wrapped around me. I looked up from the floor and saw something on the wall: an emergency cord.

Do I pull it or not? What do I really want to do here? At that moment, I didn't want the feeling of abiding peace to end. It was my chance to survive, but I was not in a rush. I didn't reach up fast and yank it, begging anyone to come. I don't know if it took me one second to pull that cord or five years. Suddenly, time didn't matter. I don't know how long it was before I reached for that cord; I just know I pulled it. Then I sank back into the blood.

Possibly a few seconds later (again, hard to know since time wasn't operational in that hospital bathroom), I looked up at what appeared to be a punk rock angel in the doorway. I know the Bible describes angels as mighty heavenly warriors. But I can tell you right now exactly what this one looked like: she was a slender, spiky bleach blonde with hair to the sky, lashes for days, and coral lipstick. Gorgeous. Glamorous. The hospital shift had changed, which meant the student nurse had gone home, and I finally got someone who would do more than try to placate me.

"Honey?" She reached down to me. "You okay?" When I

saw her, time shifted back. She was moving to the normal beat of the earth.

"I'm dying." I said once again. I'd said those words so much, I didn't expect them to have more of an impact now. They were all I had. This time, someone listened. She gently pulled me up and put me in bed and assessed the situation.

"You're not dying," she said. "But this baby is coming."

What was happening? The doctor hadn't induced me, but had I been in labor the whole time?

"He's already crowning," she said. "Another ten minutes and you would've been giving birth in that toilet. Let's go."

Let's go? I'd just been outside the realm of time, and here it was exerting its demands. But now that I was "back," I fell into step too.

The nurse grabbed a random doctor off the floor—a complete stranger to me because she wasn't in my obstetrician's practice. But before I knew it, she was helping me bring my baby into this world.

"Are you ready?" she asked me.

"Am I going to get an epidural?"

"We're gonna try." The doctor looked at my progress and frowned. "Not enough time for it to take effect."

There's a window of time—that word again—in which it's safe to get an epidural, but I'd missed the window for relief. I'd heard of women having natural births, but that's not a decision I would've made in other circumstances. In fact, I didn't make the decision in this circumstance. The baby was coming, and now that time had reengaged for me, I had to obey its strict commands.

"You've been hemorrhaging. You had gigantic blood clots in your sac. They busted, which explains all the blood."

Blood clots? They hadn't seen clots in any of the ultrasounds.

The doctor checked me again, and suddenly a gaggle of specialists, neonatal intensive care nurses, and doctors came into the room. It was like the whole cast of *Grey's Anatomy* had shown up to help, scurrying around me. (Unfortunately, there was no Dr. McDreamy or Dr. McSteamy to be found!) One of the doctors held a big glass jar.

All the doctors, nurses, and specialists who had rushed into the room indicated there was a problem with delivery, but I didn't have time to figure that out. Another pain surged through me.

"Okay, he's coming out," the doctor said. "Let's do this together."

I pushed, without my family there. Once. Twice. Then, our baby, whom we'd decided to name Blanton, arrived in this world! He'd been there, of course, for the past seven months. But now he was here for everyone to see and admire. And he was a tiny, beautiful little thing.

Everything after that was as textbook as a birth that almost occurred on the hospital toilet could be. They took my placenta and put it in that jar to study it in their efforts to figure out what had just happened. The doctors whisked away Blanton, and there I was feeling every inch of that hospital room pressing down on me. Alone.

Thirty minutes later, Travis and my family arrived. I was so relieved to see them, and now the postbirth chaos took hold.

My family members were taking turns going two at a time to the NICU to see Blanton. All eyes were on the baby, chatting and carrying on. I wasn't engaged in all that. I was still thinking about what had happened in the bathroom. I was trying to relive that moment, to feel that incredible peace again. *Did I just have a near-death experience? Did I just have an experience with God?*

Then I was jolted back to the real world with this single thought: *What if someone needs to use the bathroom?* It looked like a murder scene in there!

"Can someone clean the bathroom?" I asked the nurse. This question—to me—symbolizes what it's like to be a woman. There I was, having just escaped death and having brought life into the world, and I was worried about protecting others from what I'd just experienced. "It looks like a scene from that horror movie *Carrie*."

The nurse laughed. She was used to seeing blood, but my family, in-laws, and extended family weren't. Especially not *my* blood.

"Please, get somebody to clean that up. Please don't let people go into that bathroom with it looking like that." I said this a half dozen times. "Did you get somebody to clean that bathroom?"

As someone went to clean, probably just to shut me up, my doctor pulled a chair next to my bed.

"I can't explain this. You had three or four blood clots." He used his hands to show an approximate size of softballs. Because of my pregnancy complications, I'd had more ultrasounds than normal. I bet I had five in the past month, because they were constantly monitoring the baby. But the clots didn't show up in any of the ultrasounds, and they easily could've gone to my heart or to Blanton.

"Kim, we don't know how or why you or your baby are alive."

But I knew why.

When I was on that bloody bathroom floor, God intervened. I was not in control of anything. I didn't suddenly lose control; I realized I never had any control of that situation to begin with.

Giving birth is a miracle no matter what. But me giving birth after facing death was something else. I want to call it magical, but not like a fairy godmother or a guy pulling a bunny out of a hat. No, I'm talking about the "deeper magic" that C. S. Lewis wrote about in the Chronicles of Narnia—the magic that defeats death itself.[2]

This experience made my faith more real because I got to see life and death up close—one path led to the grave; the other one led to vitality. It was like I saw the two paths laid out before me, without knowing which path I would be able to pursue. The powerlessness I felt caused me to pause and reflect.

Why was I created?

Do I have worth?

Absolutely! I felt an enormous surge of worth, which might sound strange. God's attention was on me, and it was better than any gaze my loving parents must've lavished on me as an infant. It seems like the world conspires to rob a person of that intimate knowledge of their worth. The world is a confidence-sucker. But in that moment, I felt God's love and adoration, and worth was a natural byproduct of that. It took this experience to collect the lasting confidence in who He is. He is omnipresent, omniscient, omnipotent. If He could meet me on that bloody bathroom floor and send me that rock 'n' roll angel nurse, then He will do that for you too.

Who would have thought I'd experience deep confidence in God and an unshakable sense of worth in a hospital bathroom? Just goes to show you that God can reach you anywhere!

I may have been in the hospital, but right there on that bloody bathroom floor, I received divine revelation in what God was and is. In my life, and maybe yours, we spend a lot of time talking about faith in terms of right and wrong, sin and salvation. But when the pedal hits the metal, we realize how simple it is and how complicated we make it. God is love. And 1 John 4:18 beautifully tells us, "There is no fear in love. But perfect love drives out fear." After I let go of the fear, I began to contemplate my own life. Even though my life was spared, I realized, *I'm only here for a little bit, and what am I contributing?*

Suddenly I realized that everything was about me, and nothing was about me. God designed me and made me the way I am; I had no control over who I was created to be. In that moment, I let go of all my presuppositions about the way my life should look. I gave up my pride, my control, planning, strength, stress, anxiety, and fear. I gave up feeling guilty about things I'd done or ways I fell short. I realized this mess is my message.

I was face-to-face with it. I met my Maker that day, and He met me right where I was, broken, human, and afraid. When I was lying on the floor, I asked myself, *If I get out of this, what am I going to do with the rest of the time I have left?*

You don't have to have a near-death experience to ask that question. God created you. He adores you. And the truth is the

God created you.
He adores you.
And the truth is
the world needs
more of who you
are and what you
have to offer.

world needs more of who you are and what you have to offer.. Your individual struggles pale in comparison to that love. So why are you letting them hold you back?

One caveat. Don't give in to the shame-game. Drop the shame, the blame, and simply ask: "God, please help me!" That's what I did, and He saved my life and my son's life. Say the words and let the wonder begin.

Acknowledging your need for God does something interesting. It means you can stop playing God. Then you can do as I did: submit to Him 1000 percent. Sometimes these dire circumstances do what normal life cannot—force you to your knees. I only relinquished control over my life because I had no choice.

Hopefully, you aren't fighting a life-and-death battle. Maybe you are. Life is hard. But ideally whatever you are going through will activate your faith. Faith requires action, but I'm not talking about a to-do list. You don't have to do everything right to be loved, accepted, or have an impact. You just have to ask.

In that hospital, I asked God for help and received it. What do you need help for right now? What situation are you in that you have no control over? I wouldn't wish on anyone what happened to me, but I do wonder if we all had that experience, if we'd more easily resist the demands of our busy schedules, focus on God, and discern our calling—knowing God gives confidence you can truly count on.

And don't give in to desperation and the lie that you have wasted too much time. You haven't. God controls time—He can speed it up or slow it down. As St. Augustine wrote, "What time could there be that You had not created? Or how could ages pass, if they never were? Thus . . . You are the Maker of all times."[3]

As women, we feel we never have enough time. Time is a brutal taskmaster, harder than any sergeant in the army yelling at the newly shaved recruits. Our lives are governed by it, especially when you're trying to get the kids out the door to school, or you're trying to get your materials ready for a presentation, or you're trying to make sure you spend time with your loved ones before they run out of time on this earth.

Time, as hard a taskmaster as it seems, is not your boss.

Time, as hard a taskmaster as it seems, is not your boss. It should not have control over you. It's just something God made, something that—like the waves in the sea—obeys His commands. And when He chooses to act, He is not bound by your watch or that clock on your iPhone.

I didn't tell anyone any of this in the hospital that day, mainly because I didn't have the energy. But I am telling you now. The next time you feel all alone, you might cry out to an uncaring world, *I'm hurting. This isn't right. God, please help me.*

Help is coming. Look for it with eager anticipation.

Let Your Soul Glow!

1. God is always speaking to you. Get still and listen.
2. Be open to the miracles around you.
3. Practice celebrating others; your time will come.
4. There's a big difference between price and value. You were bought with a price because you have great value.
5. Always (always!) honor your value.

6. Live your life in the little moments.
7. Give yourself grace.
8. Encourage yourself!
9. Keep your heart toward God; your performance will catch up.
10. When God says yes, don't say no.

Eight

All-You-Can-Eat Buffet

Seize the moment. Remember all those women on the Titanic *who waved off the dessert cart.*

—Erma Bombeck

After a near-death experience, some believe they have to live life to the fullest or get busy because they never know how much time they have left. All of sudden, there's a desire to live more quickly—to do more, be more, and accomplish more. Others might have the opposite reaction and be encouraged to stop and smell the roses.

I had neither.

Almost dying did change me, but in a totally different and unexpected way: I was awed by the vastness of life. After bathing in God's presence, I realized life is a wide-open space. No longer did God occupy a certain box in my mind; He revolutionized my thoughts. No longer did I try to find my narrow slot in the world; He opened up the *whole* world. Life was more hopeful, more empowering, and bigger than I ever imagined.

That revelation could've made me feel small and puny. I've heard a lot of sermons about how insignificant we are compared to God. But God's loving glory is generous, so plentiful He embedded it into the mountains, the galaxies, and in me as well. In you too. I was bigger, bolder, and stronger than I had ever felt before. I was more assertive because God was larger, richer, and more abundant than my limited flannelgraph (Bible story paper dolls stuck to a felt background) Sunday school–inspired imagination had allowed me to believe.

When I had that near-death experience, God flipped my script. Now I wanted to be more, have more, and love harder. I wanted everyone to experience it too. I now knew His offerings are an all-you-can-eat buffet. No more playing it small.

> The crumb mentality is when we think there isn't enough to go around.

Up until this point I had hustled to get ahead. To hustle is to live small. To do almost anything to get ahead. To tell people what they want to hear but never lie. To get out and grind like your life depends on it. This is what I like to call the "crumb" mentality. The crumb mentality is when we think there isn't enough to go around—because the world is limited—that we have to press, push, and scrape to get our part of whatever's out there.

But when I was in that hospital, lying on that blood-stained floor, the bigness of life penetrated my bones. And just like that, my crumb mentality dissipated. I no longer attempted to "get what was mine," but I relaxed into the divine nature given to me by a God who assured me in 1 John 4:4 that "greater is he that is in you, than he that is in the world" (KJV).

Crumb mentality is like arguing with another person over a thimbleful of water without realizing you're sitting in a boat on the Great Lakes. This occurred to me one day as I was contemplating all that happened to me in the hospital. And somehow, that understanding also included an epiphany of my great worth. Once I had that, I stopped looking to people to help me and started to look within to discern my calling.

Here's what happened.

"We should film a reality TV show," I blurted. The members of Beloved were sitting down between sessions at a women's retreat in 2013, eating a boxed lunch that included a ham sandwich and a cookie.

"That came outta nowhere," Amy said. "About *what*, exactly?"

"We could tell our story." I took a bite of my sandwich and didn't wait until I finished chewing to continue. "People would eat that up."

She looked at me blankly. "Us? Just singing? Who's gonna watch almost-middle-aged women, pursuing a music career and a record deal? No one's gonna want to watch that."

"Sure, they will!" I said. "We can call the show *Sagging but Not Dragging*."

Amy laughed and tilted her head in consideration, but I didn't wait to hear whatever protest might be coming next.

"We just need to find out how to create a reality TV show."

Amy went to the computer and entered into the search engine: "How do you create a reality TV show?"

No lie.

The next week, we went to lunch, and she said, "Looks like we need a sizzle reel."

"What's that?"

She read from the screen on her phone, where she'd created a checklist. "It's an attention-grabbing video, from two to five minutes, showing a proof of concept." She looked up at me. "Like a movie trailer."

Over the next few months we hired some people to shoot footage while we sang and talked to the ladies at our women's conferences. We shot one short video of us, dressed all in black, talking and joking with each other. We got dressed up, poked fun at ourselves, flashed our girdles, and laughed. The video was raw and real and totally us. We'd shot it in one of our unfinished basements using flashlights as our "natural light." The final result was homegrown but got the point across!

In my video, we also featured Travis and the kids, because you don't know me unless you know them. I stared down camera lens and stated that I needed to lose fifty pounds but was hesitant to lose weight. "I'm a lady with a purpose," I said. "I don't have time to figure all that mess out." Plus, I liked my junk in the trunk and my curves. (Okay, maybe I'd try to lose twenty pounds.) "I don't always like everything I am, but I'm everything God made me to be, and I like myself. I'm about making sure everyone finds out who God has made them to be."

That was that. I was real. I was me.

"What do we do now?" I asked Amy.

"Now we have to send this sizzle reel to a production company." She looked at me. "Know anyone at a production company?"

I wanted the right partner, so I went back to the internet and googled "production companies that create reality television shows." About ten thousand results popped up.

We didn't know what we were doing yet. But I was tired of the "I'm too afraid, too tired, or don't know how" excuses. I'd never again say "I can't" or "I'm too small." I had a new frame of mind: when God calls you to do something, nothing can stop it, damage it, alter it, or prevent it—except you.

So we sent out our sizzle reel blindly to over four hundred production companies that first day. Weeks passed. No one replied. Then, we learned about something called the slush pile, the place where unsolicited material goes, and figured no one ever saw it.

Eventually, a guy named Oliver Bogner responded. Little did we know Oliver was barely out of braces, a Hollywood wunderkind. He was like sixteen years old, but we didn't know it. We eagerly agreed to let him pitch our reel, sat back, and waited.

This might sound unwise or reckless to you, but I just started trying things. I didn't always know what to do or how to take action, but I knew if I put one foot in front of the other—just took one step—that what I felt called to do would not fail me.

Maybe I made some mistakes, but I had to get moving. I knew God would make a way. It didn't matter how old I was,

When God calls you to do something, nothing can stop it, damage it, alter it, or prevent it—except you.

that I was an almost-middle-aged woman seeking to do a reality television show and share the message that we can all have a big life. We really wanted people to know that a woman of any age could express her gifts and live out her calling in a bold, authentic, fearless way. And maybe people would find that interesting and inspiring. Not to mention hilarious! Keep in mind I already had my pantyhose explode onstage, so who knows what would happen on reality TV.

I was ready to grab hold of whatever God had in store. The world is a confidence sucker, remember, but I had been infused with a spirit of courage and adventure. You've heard of the Salvation Army? Well, I'd joined the "Vocation Army" and was in boot camp.

Until now I never widely pursued anything without trying to be perfect: perfect weight, perfect image, perfect hair, perfect manners. But y'all, calling does not equal perfection; it equals fulfillment. At the end of the day, we're all just looking to be fulfilled. We want to be perfect because we think perfection will make us valuable. But what we're seeking is not external value equating to things we do. It's not performance based. What we long for is fulfillment, being fully developed in our abilities and character. That's what living out your calling does. It fills you up and then overflows to others.

"What you do" is all the actionable things—volunteer at a soup kitchen, write a book, help a friend. The "why you do what you do" is the calling behind it. Sometimes we get these things confused. What I do is reality TV, building brands, and writing books. But why I do these things is to build people up.

The "what you do" might change from one year to the next—heck, from one hour to the next. But the "why you do" never alters. Up until this point I was focusing on the what and not the why.

If you can define your calling, it's unshakable. But defining it is key. My friend Amy drilled her calling down to "I want to bring order." Mine is to edify. I'm supposed to lift people up with my message, so I was willing to do it with everything . . . yes, even if that's a reality television show. Once I realized that calling, big things opened up for me.

A few weeks later, Oliver the teenage producer called.

If God could use a donkey in the Bible to speak, as He did in Numbers 22:28–30, He could use a Gen-Z wunderkind teenager who hadn't even graduated high school to help me with my calling. Why not? I put Oliver on speaker.

"I've been doing a soft pitch to people in the industry to get their feedback," he said. "Great news! Everyone loves you. You have an amazing personality and really jump off the screen." He specifically said my video piqued their interest. "But no one is interested in a show about older ladies seeking a record deal."

Amy reached over and hit me on the arm. "I told you."

"Stop it," I mouthed.

When Oliver told me no one was interested in our original pitch, a whole other door opened for me—just a crack at first—when he asked, "What else do you have going on?"

Never ask me that unless you got time.

So I told Oliver that over the years I helped young women prepare for pageants. I'd had the Nancys, my mom, and my mentors help me in my pageants, so I paid it forward. My mom, sister, and I—with a combined sixty-plus years of pageant and coaching experience—know what it takes to produce winners, and they don't have to look like models to do it. We know how to bring the best out of each girl—including runway walk, talent, platform development, interview preparation, wardrobe consulting, hair/makeup consulting, bio prep, stage presence, and much more. But our focus was to see each girl develop her unique potential.

If at first you don't succeed, pivot. I would say 100 percent of the time, the opportunity never looks like what you imagined it to be. Whatever you're dreaming of, don't get too attached to what it looks like. Keep your "why" front and center. I can guarantee you, with the greatest authority, your "what you do" is going to change and change often.

If at first you don't succeed, pivot.

"Might be something there," he said. "Can you create a sizzle reel for that?"

I went to Mom and Allisyn and floated the idea. "We're going to film a reality TV show."

Allisyn didn't even look up. "Okay," she said.

"So, you're in?"

"You're serious?" She cocked her head at me. Allisyn is the type of person made for reality television. She talks nonstop about topics as deep as a puddle, and she's apt to throw a glass of wine in your face if you look at her sideways. She's up for anything and is the life of the party. There'd be no party without her. She's great for the drama, but she's also very loyal and has a heart as big as Texas. She sees the best in people, which would make her perfect for pulling the best out of these young girls.

"Why would I bring it up if I wasn't serious?"

"Sometimes you get some ideas going, and I never know what to think," she said. "And we get on the train with you, and then you stop rolling down those tracks. You get off the train and are off to do something else."

"That's a bold-faced lie," I said, "and you know it. You in or out?"

"I'm in, honey!" Allisyn said. I could tell she was excited.

"What about you, Mom?" I asked.

She stirred some sugar in her coffee slowly, blew on it, and took a sip. "I don't understand why you want to do another TV show, Kim. Are you just trying to get back at me for *In the Heat of the Night*?"

In the Heat of the Night was a crime drama starring Carroll O'Connor as police chief that ran from 1988 until 1995. When I was a kid, they shot some of the episodes in Conyers, Georgia, and one of the producers had seen me singing in a pageant. He called Mom and offered me a part—not an audition, but an actual role.

Mom didn't even consult with me, because she didn't want to immerse me in show business so early in life. She told him I wasn't available, then later casually mentioned the opportunity to me. I lost it. I couldn't imagine anything cooler than being on a top-rated show as a kid, but Mom was resolute. "I have a life, Kim; I can't run you up and down the road to a TV show set."

Sometimes a "no" is a "not yet."

Sometimes a "no" is a "not yet." If I had been in *In the Heat of the Night*, my life would have been different. It was a sparkling opportunity that ultimately would have been a distraction and prevented me from becoming the person I am today. Plus, I'm not sure Mom thought too deeply about it. She probably just didn't want to miss her Wednesday night suppers at church and the gospel sing-along.

But when I brought up the idea of a reality TV show to Mom, she didn't get hysterical; she got historical. I couldn't believe she'd bring up that show so many years later. I looked at my mother and rolled my eyes. "This has nothing to do with *In the Heat of the Night,* but let the record show I'm still mad at you over that," I said jokingly. In my heart, I knew she had the best intentions for me.

Mom is perfect for reality TV for different reasons than Allisyn. She couldn't care less about frivolous things. Her conversation goes straight to the heart of deep matters. Mom loves confrontation and isn't afraid to use it to resolve issues quickly. She'll verbally slap you upside the head in Jesus' name.

Mom agreed to shoot the sizzle reel, and the next day, my sister Allisyn, my mom, and I sat at my house with Amy behind her iPhone camera. Instead of hiring someone to create a stylized production, the three of us just talked to one another, fought with one another, and insulted one another as we talked about the art of the pageant. When we get together, it's always a lot of fun. So we decided to simply just do what we do.

Would you believe Oliver singlehandedly got me that show? Lifetime loved it, and the idea for my reality television show, *Kim of Queens*, was born. The premise was simple: the show would follow Allisyn, Mom, and me at our family-owned business called The Pageant Place. There, we would train girls to feel comfortable in their skin, to walk confidently even when they were scared, and to simply be their best.

Suddenly, I had a national platform, and my name was all over everything. This pulled back the veil and let me think about what was important for me. Fame? Money? What did I want? My "why" was always very clear. It was always to get this message out to everyone: "The world needs what you have to offer."

I was just putting into practice what my parents taught Allisyn and me but applied to the modern world. Kids today face so much more than we had to face as children, with all the social media bombarding them. Our young people get the same message over and over from the culture: conform. The girls are told the definition of beauty is being slim, , being tall, and having clear skin, big lips, full breasts, and lush lashes. They're told the definition of success is to have money, a big house, a flashy car, designer clothes, and a private jet. These lies kill kids' creativity and confidence, expose them to things that they shouldn't be exposed to at an early age, keep them from developing their own personalities, and divert them from walking in their calling.

Beauty is not a shape, size, age, or skin color.

I wanted the pageant contestants to know that beauty and success are specific to each person. Beauty is not a shape, size, age, or skin color. I wanted them to learn what I learned on the floor of the hospital. They were already beautiful; they just had to walk in it.

Lots of times—in life and in pageants—we look at other people and covet what they have. But competition with other women kills. I wanted to teach them that you are only in competition with yourself. The goal is to work hard and be your authentic self. Pageants have gotten a bad rap and are perceived as frivolous, focused more on outward appearances than intelligence and talent. It all matters! I wanted to use pageants as a backdrop to give the girls permission to be confident in their own skin and their own beauty—in the totality of who they are. The skills of pageantry have utility in actual life. Pageants can teach girls how to speak, cultivate an opinion, and know what they believe and why they believe it. The skills I would teach them would help them way beyond the stage.

"Isn't this sweet?" my producer said one day after we began filming. "You'll be able to show your grandkids this series." I just smiled and nodded, thinking, *He's as lost as an Easter egg.* I knew in my soul that this was going to be much bigger than a glorified scrapbook for my family. *Oh no, baby, this is just an appetizer.*

We tend to approach life with an "à la carte" attitude, thinking, *I can have one of those and just a little of that,* when life is a full-on all-you-can-eat buffet, dessert included! Our opportunities are limited only by our mindset. But when you collect confidence, you have the courage to receive life's richness. My grandma Blanton used to say, "Live like wine or live like milk. One gets better with age. The other gets lumpy and smelly. It's yours to decide." Baby, I'd decided. *Kim of Queens* was going to be a huge moment for me, even if people didn't believe me.

Belief is one thing, but the work has to get done. The hard work is worth it, because by doing it you discover you are made for more. Getting anywhere takes work and it takes stamina! Stamina means you can withstand the hard times with resilience and steadfastness. When I was competing for Miss

Georgia, my dad told me, "You need to build enough stamina to get through five days of competition." And that's what I did—one day at a time, sweet Jesus! The last girl standing wins Miss America. Don't look to the left; don't look to the right; stay your course.

Doing *Kim of Queens* required resilience too—for me, my family, and the girls in the show. The Pageant Place contestants were beautiful and amazing, but I wasn't trying to create little Barbies. I wasn't really trying to produce pageant winners. I wanted to create future leaders. I wanted them to get from point A to Z, with enough confidence to accomplish their life's success.

But it ain't reality TV without a little drama. (Who am I kidding? The drama is why I watch *Real Housewives*!) On *Kim of Queens*, the behind-the-scenes stuff was even better than what viewers saw. It changed all our lives.

One of my favorite moments was with a contestant named Addison, a country girl who cleaned up real nice. The thing I loved about Addison was her gun-toting, hunting ways. She didn't know enough to be intimidated, and she put a lot of effort into making things right. But when I was preparing her to participate in a big pageant in Nashville, I needed her to work on her dancing. When I took her to the studio, I surprised her with Lance Bass, an international pop star. She absolutely freaked out. She couldn't talk at first, because she was a big NSYNC fan. Finally, with her hands over her face, she said to Lance, "Do you know who you are?"

He laughed and asked her, "Do *you* know who *you* are?"

That's a good question for all of us. It was the question I wanted the girls to contemplate, win or lose. "Winning Miss

"Winning Miss Georgia was fantastic," I told one of the girls. "But losing Miss America taught me more. It's the failures that make you who you are. Not the wins."

Georgia was fantastic," I told one of the girls. "But losing Miss America taught me more. It's the failures that make you who you are, not the wins."

Sometimes the girls' lives were complicated. One fan favorite was my dear friend Deb, whom I've known for twenty years. She was known as "Barbie Mama," and her daughter Hannah looked just like her. She had big, bleached blonde hair, pink lipstick, the works. As we filmed, I noticed Hannah was shrinking right before my eyes. She was getting thinner and thinner—she wasn't big to begin with—and the fans and cast worried too. Once another mother saw Hannah's jeans hanging off her bones and pulled on her waistband. "Girl, what's going on?"

I asked if Hannah had an eating disorder. Finally, Deb softened and admitted Hannah was anorexic. The guilt was crushing her. "This is not your fault." I reached over and put my hand on hers. "But I'm not going to let Hannah be on the show until you guys get her back on track. Deb, you have to get Hannah some help."

Hannah went to get help when the show went on hiatus, and the next season she was able to talk more comfortably about her struggles. She decided she even wanted to talk about it on camera.

"Are you sure?" I asked. I knew this would be such a big moment for such a little girl.

But she insisted, and it truly was a game changer—not only for her but also for the viewers at home.

I love that we were able to include that story in the show, because I wanted the young girls who watched the show to see that struggles can be the most amazing, confidence-building moments you will ever have in your life. These situations can set you on your destiny path. You make choices in life, but sometimes choices make you.

Hannah made the choice to get help and heal and then shared her brave act in the most public way with the hope it would help others. And boy, did it help a lot of people. Hannah took a step forward. You can do it too. It's okay to start small. Just start! As Zechariah 4:10 tells us, "Do not despise these small beginnings, for the LORD rejoices to see the work begin" (NLT).

You make choices in life but sometimes choices make you.

We all grew in so many ways while making the show, and many people grew up while watching it. If just one person took these sorts of lessons from the show, that would've made the show a success, worth all the work and the long days. There will be challenges, and people might tell you your dream is silly. But trust your calling. That's what I did. I put one thing out into the world and then another. Everything has a season, and *Kim of Queens* was not renewed for a third season. But in life's buffet you can always go back for seconds. The beautiful thing about an all-you-can-eat buffet is that you can try something you never tried before—it doesn't cost extra.

Everyone needs a personal mission statement about your calling. What is your calling? Is it to heal, to inspire, to create? The more you can drill down your calling into two or three words, the more limitless your opportunities. My calling is to edify, to build up. It's expressed many different ways—in my relationships, my jobs, my parenting, and my conversations.

We limit ourselves by thinking there are only so many

opportunities out there for each of us, but God is limitless. He is abundant. Stop with your à la carte mentality. You can only be as big as your smallest thought, but your calling is big. Unleash your limiting beliefs.

No one can do what you're made to do. No one else has what you have. When you operate in your giftedness, things and people can try to knock you down. But nothing can stop it. If you have the desire, do the work, and are confident in your calling, the opportunities will show up for you. It will take some patience to wait for them and it will take stamina to walk in them.

You can only be as big as your smallest thought, but your calling is big. Unleash your limiting beliefs.

I wish I could just walk up to you and show you how absolutely magnificent you are. But that's why I'm writing this book. So take it from me: you are fearfully and wonderfully made. Quit looking at the problem as being really big, and start looking at your calling as being really big. Big isn't going to be easy, and it's going to be work. Trust me, if it doesn't look like you imagined, it'll be better.

I was trying to secure a reality TV show based on middle-aged women trying to get a record deal. I never imagined a pageant-related show. And it was so much better than what I had dreamed up.

You can have a big life too. Remember that it's an all-you-can-eat buffet. Fill up your plate. You can go back to the smorgasbord of life over and over again. Don't have an a la carte mentality. I can have a little of this and some of that. You can always go back for more. Whatever you're thinking about doing, if it doesn't scare you, you're not thinking big enough.

Life is an all you can eat buffet, y'all, and it's good.

So dig in!

Queen for a Day: Beauty Tips and Tricks

1. To wear high heels for three hours straight pain free, tape your pinky toe to the toe beside it.

2. For the perfect cleavage, apply body tape (I use duct tape) across your chest to bring your breasts together. This technique can also be used as a minimizer.

4. Wear white on special occasions. It gives you the halo glow effect.

6. Stand with your head, shoulders, butt, and heels flush against the wall for five minutes daily for better posture.

Bonus: How to answer any question and sound brilliant. Always do these three things:

- *Answer the question:*

  Q: Is it possible to have world peace?

  A: Yes, I think it's possible to have world peace.
- *Tell why:*

  It's possible to have world peace because I believe that people are good at heart.
- *Give an example:*

  I was recently in the grocery store, standing in line and holding a few items. The woman in front of me had a cart full of groceries, and she said to me, "Do you want to go ahead of me? You only have a few items and I have a full cart."

If you answer any question like this in a pageant or any public arena, you'll win. That's a tip you can take into your life forever.

Nine

Level Up, Buttercup!

To thine own self be true, and it must follow, as the night the day, thou canst not then be false to any man.

—William Shakespeare

The heat wafted from the stove as the grease in the skillet started bubbling. I covered my pork chops in a flour mixture and placed them carefully in the pan. I was looking in the fridge to see what else I had to serve for dinner, when my phone rang.

"Great news," my agent said. "Someone who works with QVC has reached out about you doing a line on their network."

My heart leaped, then sank. I'd worked with this agent for a while and wanted my own QVC line for many years. In early

2006, I dreamed and even had a vision that I wanted to have a cosmetic brand of my own on QVC. My mom and all her friends were watchers and shoppers on QVC to the point the UPS delivery man knew my mom by name. I dreamed of going on a live show at QVC and the "Sold Out" sign popping up on the screen. So, after *Kim of Queens* was canceled, I started working on a skincare moisturizer called Aloemend and a lip plumper lip gloss in hopes my agent could get me a meeting.

We had been working together for more than three years, but I just wasn't sure he was the right fit for me. He wanted me to change the way I talk. He didn't want me to talk in southern colloquialisms all the time.

Was he worried that I wouldn't sound smart enough for a meeting like this? My mind raced as that sliver of doubt lodged in my brain. But I thanked him and got off the phone. I called Amy.

"You aren't going to believe this." I flipped the pork chops over in the pan.

"What's wrong?" She could tell from my voice that I wasn't okay. I tried to quickly explain the opportunity I feared I couldn't take.

"Slow down." Her voice was calm. "This is not the right time. You are moving on from your agent. It's just not the right time or the right people. If it's meant to be, this opportunity will find you again."

Easier said than done. Because it was a huge opportunity. One that comes along maybe once in a lifetime.

I began to cry so hard, my tears dropped into the frying pan. Each drop of grief, sizzling and popping, cried out for my attention. I knew what I had to do.

I called my agent back and told him not to set up the meeting.

I hung up the phone, took my overdone pork chops out, and placed them on a platter. They grew cold as I sat down at the table and wept.

All I could think about was the lost opportunity. *Had I done the right thing?*

A few months later, Amy and I flew to California so I could record Steve Harvey's show. I had first appeared on his show when I was promoting *Kim of Queens,* and I was fortunate enough to be asked back as a regular contributor. Amy and I were sitting in the hotel lobby, waiting for the car service to pick us up. A television flickered above the mantelpiece, families pulled luggage on brass carts, and I absentmindedly scrolled through Twitter.

"Amy." I couldn't tear my eyes away from my screen.

She looked up from her own phone and grabbed her purse. "Is the car here?"

I shoved my phone in her face, showing her a tweet that popped up in my mentions. Amy read it aloud. "Was watching Jane Treacy on QVC and she just mentioned that she's a huge #KimofQueens fan."

She looked at me, her eyes wide in disbelief. "Jane Treacy knows who you are?"

"More than that! She's a fan of *Kim of Queens*!" I corrected her. Jane was barely twenty-four years old when she started her more than two-decade run on QVC. Fans love the way she speaks from the heart, no teleprompter needed. Jane Treacy, a QVC host, was talking about *me*! Maybe this opportunity hadn't forgotten about me.

Many times, when you're in a period of waiting, it feels like no one in the world even knows you're alive. It might even feel like God isn't working or watching.

That's because—as humans—we're stuck in this thing called time. We can't see the big picture. When we're suffering, it might feel like it's the end of the world, but we can't perceive what's really going on. We feel like we're trapped in a perpetual slow-motion loop, but things are going on behind the scenes we can't see. Opportunities are lining up, the right people coming into view.

Are you in a time loop? Do you feel like Bill Murray starring in your own *Groundhog Day* movie? Every day you feel invisible, sad, and hopeless. You might feel overlooked. You might feel forgotten. But remember that timing makes a difference. Some answers must wait, and—while you're in that waiting period—remember that God is writing your story and He's a much better author than you and I put together. God's always moving.

Sometimes you have to walk away from an opportunity that seems good to wait for what's best.

Sometimes you have to walk away from an opportunity that seems good to wait for what's best. You don't have to live in the good; you can wait for the best. When you can't work your way to an opportunity, you feel it's your only shot and it's passing you by. You start to feel desperate, which makes you feel powerless.

Let me share a secret with you: the "power wait."

Power waiting is an antidote to the desperation of the

hustle culture. God doesn't hustle. Hustling is all about seizing every second, hurrying every day, and taking advantage of every so-called opportunity. But God doesn't need opportunity. He *is* opportunity! He doesn't have to hustle, and neither do you. Romans 8:25 says, "But if we hope for what we do not yet have, we wait for it patiently." I've wasted so much time, emotional energy, and money trying to make things happen. What is meant for you will find you. It will show up. You don't have to beg for it. You don't have to settle or just take what's offered.

That meant I didn't have to tie myself into knots to make this happen. Sometimes the only work you need to do is wait. But this was the hardest thing I've ever done. I don't know about you, but when I'm waiting for something to happen, I sometimes feel lost and ignored—like I could disappear, and no one would notice. But time spent waiting can be more valuable than instant success.

How do you power wait?

Accept it.

Trust the timing.

Don't try to force an opportunity.

Prepare for it.

Wait in anticipation for it.

Be patient, like your mama always said. Have enough faith and confidence that what you bring to that opportunity will be utilized. Know that when you're operating in your calling, the opportunity will find you at the right moment.

But while you're power waiting, you can prepare patiently. And—this is important—use that time waiting to be ready when an opportunity presents itself. Believe it's happening, but the fact that you don't have it yet means more preparation is needed. Prepare for it like it's already coming. As one of my favorite scriptures says, "Faith is the substance of things hoped for, the evidence of things not seen" (Hebrews 11:1 KJV). I've always been taught that God has three answers to our prayers: "yes," "not yet," or "I've got something better." The hardest thing for me, and for all of us I believe, is accepting or abiding in what that answer is. If it is "not yet" or "I've got something better," then it requires power waiting. And so I waited. And waited. It felt like years, but three months later after I turned down the QVC opportunity and the thirty-day waiting period to separate from my agent had expired, almost to the day, a manufacturer working with QVC for over thirty years reached out to me.

The opportunity found me again, and we scheduled a meeting.

Amy and I excitedly chatted in the cab, which was taking us from LaGuardia to—as the old Pace Picante ads said—"Neeew York City" for meetings with the independent companies who manufacture for QVC.

"Are we *really* in New York for a meeting for your brands to appear on QVC?" Amy muted the taxi's TV screen loudly playing an ad for the Broadway musical *Wicked*.

"We should try to see that show before we leave," I said.

We both stopped talking when the New York skyline appeared on the horizon, and I pressed my face to the window. The skyscrapers glistened, even though there was an overcast sky that the sun jutted through like a catfish on a line. We had traveled together many times, especially to the West Coast, but Manhattan had an awe-inspiring quality that emanated opportunity, wealth, and power. It took our breath away.

"I wouldn't put my face on that window," Amy said. "It's filthy." But my eyes were wide open as I wondered what would happen. Now that I was free from the constraints of my agent's contract, I could follow my dreams.

We walked into a meeting with a group of people who manufactured for QVC. They were stylish and well put together. I guess that makes sense for people interested in me pitching a line of clothing to QVC and—ultimately—starting a new brand.

I sat in a chair and glanced out the window to the busy streets in New York City. It was daunting. I'm sitting in a showroom in the middle of the fashion district talking about creating a fashion line. *How did I get here?*

I never in my wildest dreams even thought about being in the fashion business. But remember, don't get too attached to the "what" you do. What you do is always fluid. Be open to the pivot. This was only my first step toward actually making it on QVC. What I really wanted to do was a beauty and skincare line.

First, I had to get my foot in the door.

"I could get you on the air in six months," said one manufacturer. "I can see your show now in my head. We should do it as soon as possible."

"Hmm, not sure about that." A manufacturer named Susan shook her head. "That's way too fast. We don't want her to be a flash in the pan." I thought back to my sizzling pork-chop tears and agreed with her. I really liked Susan. She was tall, slender, and dressed to the nines. She wasn't pretentious, wearing fancy labels. She was aspirational and classy in head-to-toe navy with the most beautiful statement ring. She sure did make a statement. I knew I had to work with her. Not to mention, I completely agreed with her. Anything worth doing is worth doing well. Hard work and preparation save everyone from heartache. I first wrote in my journal in 2007 that I wanted a brand on QVC and I had waited a long time. Honestly, what was a little more time?

During that meeting, I learned some of the behind-the-scenes chatter that caused Jane Treacy to mention me on air, the first sign of hope that this might work out. Apparently, Susan and her team were fans of *Kim of Queens*, and they began to talk about how I'd have a shot at doing well on QVC. All of that was going on behind the scenes. I hadn't hustled to get any of this attention. It all was lining up while I was waiting . . . and preparing.

"When I read that tweet, I was happier than a tornado in a trailer park," I said to Susan. "Jane Treacy knew my name."

"Not only does she know your name, but she's also dying to meet you."

Happy to meet me? Girl, God must've been cooking something up. When you're cooking, you have to have the right ingredients, right? Well, the Master Chef was cooking up my opportunity, and He brought the right people to come alongside me, which blessed them and me.

Susan dialed Jane's number and put it on speaker. When she answered, she said, "Jane, you're not going to believe who I'm with."

Jane laughed and told me how much she loved me on the show. Little did she know, I had been fan-girling over her for years! Jane Treacy is a petite firecracker, a powerhouse kind of woman. Her turns of phrase coupled with her instant BFF personality makes her the best on live TV. I'd watched her for years and was in awe at her authenticity.

"I can't believe you want to meet me," I said.

"I sure do," she said. "In fact, in my journal this year, I wrote down two people I hoped to meet: the pope and Kim Gravel."

Well, that was a short and rarified list. We chatted and laughed, and she wished me well. After a couple of hours, the meeting was over, and Amy and I walked back to our hotel in Times Square.

We were in shock from how well the meeting went. Right there on the crowded sidewalk I was taking off my three-inch heels and slipping on my no-tie sneakers.

"Anyway, what did you think about that meeting?"

"There's a difference between someone being *with* you and someone being *for* you. And I think Susan was *for* us."

I agreed. Life is too short to surround yourself with people who aren't pulling on the same oars to get to the same place. It takes the right people and the right time. So many times, we try to get people to believe in us, but not everyone will see you. Think about this. One of the best lessons I've learned personally in business and in life is that sometimes when you are rejected, told no, or get a less-than-enthusiastic response, the right thing to do might be simply to walk away. Don't waste time trying to convince people that you are right or you are enough.

Don't waste time trying to convince people that you are right or you are enough.

Once we came to terms with Susan and her company, we all began to work on our QVC pitch. I did this without an agent because I had learned how to be my own advocate. In business and in life, you must learn to be your own advocate. (Or co-advocate, because God's got your back.)

Susan's team was a small group of amazing, prolific, and creative designers. I couldn't believe that so much talent was at my fingertips. In particular, Leslie was a gifted designer. How can someone's passion and heart become a thing? Leslie's heart and passion is evident in her design, her pitches, and her work. We were sympatico. I look forward to getting up every day to work with this team of astounding women. The Belle brand was born. We are a brand for women, made by women. Our mission was clear and still is. We wanted every woman to believe in her own beauty.

First, Amy and I had familiarized ourselves with the company, so in March 2015, we took our first trip to QVC's Studio Park—a massive, nearly seventeen-acre property outside Philadelphia with more than fifty-eight-thousand square feet of filming studios.

When I walked into the building, I knew this was home for me. Everything was pristine; even the baseboards sparkled like diamonds. When we walked through Product Central, we gawked at the hundreds of thousands of items about to be featured on air: roller carts stacked with makeup, jewelry, electric chainsaws, Christmas ornaments, food processors, and leather kimono belts.

"QVC serves fourteen million active customers in seven languages across three continents," said Susan. But even though over two thousand employees worked in the modern, well-lit complex, the sets had a *from-our-living-room-to-yours* vibe.

"Do they just let anyone in here?" I heard the familiar voice behind me, only to turn around and see Jane Treacy. Don't you know I hugged that woman's neck until the life almost left her body?

That night, we dined at an Asian-inspired, French-infused restaurant in celebration. I had the best pimiento cheese wontons that exploded with flavor in my mouth. The next day, we got down to business. We had to figure out how to pitch to the many QVC executives, so we discussed all the steps we needed to take between now and the big day: we needed to develop product boards for apparel, product boards for beauty, product samples, a press kit, a marketing deck, branding artwork, and the sales pitch.

I believe in the great philosopher Yoda, who famously said, "Do. Or do not. There is no try."[1] To prepare for QVC, the entire team did the work. And so it began.

We began dreaming of clothing that would flatter every body type. We looked at styles in magazines to see what we liked and what we didn't. For over a year, we traveled back to New York and went shopping at Macy's and Nordstrom, their racks filled with beautiful clothing from which we'd find inspiration.

"Look at this blouse." I picked up a shirt and held it up for everyone to see. I saw so many beautiful clothes, but when I imagined *my* line, I knew the colors would be bright, the fabric easy to live in. We wanted to appeal to our future audience, women at home in their pj's who want to look in the mirror and love what they see.

"You'll love these." I laid a pair of jeans on the desk in front of Susan and ran my hands over the fabric. It was part yoga pant, part denim. My mom had stretchy jeans that were stretched out and worn out. One day, having lunch with her at her house, she threw them at me and said, "I want you to make jeans like these. Look like denim but feel like knit. But Kim, I can't have a saggy butt and saggy knees by noon."

"Too late," I said. "You already got 'em." We laughed.

"I'm serious," she said. "Women are looking for jeans like this but can't find them."

Susan wasted no time and got on the horn with her factories, and that's how this life-changing fabric we called Flexibelle was birthed. Of course, to this day, my mom takes all the credit.

We spent many months with fabric companies picking prints, making samples, designing tops, sweaters, and all different kinds of items to go with our Flexibelle jeans to present to QVC.

But for me, more is more. I also wanted to pitch a beauty line.

"Not sure you can pitch beauty and fashion at the same time. Generally, new brands start with one category," said Susan.

I had a decision to make. I'd seen how the ladies at numerous women's conferences transformed when they applied the right kind of makeup. They looked good and felt good. I prayed and prayed about it.

I had someone ask me one time, "Kim, can a lip gloss really change a woman's life?"

I replied, "Yes. Beauty starts on the inside, but sometimes for women if we can't see it on the outside, it's hard for us to believe it on the inside."

So I said to Susan, "It just feels right in my gut to pitch

the beauty line. I'm gonna pitch both." Another lesson learned, never doubt that gut intuition. Remember that people can't always see what you see. God gives you that vision. It might take a minute for everyone to catch up.

In September of that same year it was time to pitch this baby at the QVC offices. I hung the clothing items on a wall behind me. On the large mahogany table, I set out, for each executive, a lip kit wrapped in a gold ribbon, a little blue makeup clutch, an eye-shadow palette, and an exfoliating cloth.

I stood there in that room, with all those executives, with as much confidence as I could collect. *Could I really do this? Would they like my products? Would they like me? Was I making a career-ending mistake?*

I pitched for an hour, with all my heart sharing my "why." I wanted women everywhere to believe in their own beauty, to look in the mirror and *love* what is looking back at them. After the presentation, QVC accepted both beauty and apparel. Everybody had told me that QVC would not take both based on past experience. But that day, despite what was the norm, I walked in confidence and trusted my gut and cut a new path. My dad used to tell me, "Kim, life is a jungle; sometimes you have to pick up a machete and cut a new path for yourself."

My new apparel line would be called "Belle by Kim Gravel," and my cosmetic line would be "Belle Beauty." Now that we had settled on brand names, we needed to trademark them. Here we go!

Most people hire a trademark attorney, but not us.

"Just google 'how to apply for a trademark,'" I told Amy.

I had confidence we could take care of it ourselves. After all, Google had worked for us before. She went to work on applying for the trademark while I prepared for the launch.

But with new levels comes new devils. When you're walking in your purpose, it is a magical and exciting adventure. But an adventure can also be a hazardous activity. So was this.

Out of the blue, I was sitting at my desk, and I opened a letter from an attorney and the state of California stating that we were being sued regarding our new trademarks, Flexibelle and Belle by Kim Gravel. I read and then reread the papers. *I'm being sued? For what? Applying for a trademark?* I couldn't understand this. It was a frivolous and unfounded lawsuit, but very real. We got our trademark info from Google, but now we were going to need God . . . and a good lawyer.

Being sued packs an emotional punch. I wouldn't recommend it.

The trademark was pretty important to moving forward, and this lawsuit could stop everything. I dropped down to my knees. Travis had never seen me so despondent. We had poured every bit of our money into our launch. We didn't have a slingshot or a stone to fight this Goliath who was trying to derail us. Have you ever felt like you have an enemy, and you don't know why? You take one step forward and two steps back? Have you ever felt like when you get a little bit of goodness in your life, that everything is conspiring to knock it down, to kill it? How was I going to fight this?

"He's holding our trademarks hostage," I told Amy and Travis. "Maybe he just liked the name 'Flexibelle' and thinks his company could use it, so he's trying to bully us into giving him what he wants."

I had been so excited about my relationship with QVC, and this lawyer was threatening everything. I was afraid it might jeopardize the launch of the whole line. I hired a trademark attorney, but I didn't have extra tens of thousands of dollars lying around to burn. This lawyer was trying to shake us down, and I couldn't let that happen.

You know you're on the right path when you encounter obstacles. All that time I had been collecting confidence. *Did I trust my calling enough to fight for it?*

Yes, I did. But let me tell you I was eaten up by fear, tormented by doubt. But I believed that God does not bring you this far to leave you or take you backward. Even though I was scared to death, I chose to trust Him. Daily—hour by hour, minute by minute—I had to stretch my faith muscle. Faith and fear can exist in the same orbit; I don't care what they say. I was scared to death but in total belief that this would work out. I just had no clue how.

If you are going to live the adventure of your calling, you better be able to put up your dukes. The Notorious B.I.G. has a song called, "Mo Money, Mo Problems." That's what happened. I leveled up, and the responsibility, headaches, and obstacles ratcheted up too. But I wasn't going to be destroyed by them. I had to develop business toughness, mental toughness, and tough faith. Sometimes you have to be bold and develop a tough exterior. As we folks from the South say, "You have to nut up, y'all!"

I don't pretend to understand what lawyers do, but motions were filed, objected to, and filed again. Every time my attorney worked on this case, I knew his clock was ticking . . . and money drained out of my bank account by the hour.

I had to fight this battle for a full year. It ended up costing both parties over fifty thousand dollars, and nothing came of it.

Well, something did come from it. Not only did I learn about trademarks, lawsuits, and how much lawyers really make per hour (why didn't I become an attorney at their hourly rate?) but figured out how to learn for myself. Nothing makes you more eager to learn than when you have everything to lose. I learned that I could be creative in design, branding, and product, but that I could be stealthy and ferocious when it came to business. Y'all, you need both. I learned how to put on my big girl panties and be strategic in fighting my own battles.

Ultimately, the lawsuit was dropped. Some might look at this and think, *What a waste of time and money!* And—in a way—they'd be right. But there was something at stake that was even more valuable than money. My gumption, strength, and my "How bad do you want it?" was up for grabs. This legal battle ended up being a big ole blessing.

Now, I thank God for this legal harassment every day. Really. Refusing to give in to this harassment gave me the business shrewdness and confidence for even *bigger* levels. Your adversaries are simply sparring partners, training you for what's next.

Your adversaries are simply sparring partners, training you for what's next.

But while all of this was being worked out, I had to launch my line. I wasn't going to be intimidated. I was not going to stop. I trusted God would handle it and pushed through even before He resolved it.

Finally, the big launch day came.

On August 22, 2016, at ten o'clock in the morning, Jane Treacy hosted a segment that featured my products. It was just Jane and me for a whole hour. Jane put her neck on the line for me. She held my hand and walked me onto the QVC set. I couldn't have paid for that, and my heart raced. I would not be at QVC if not for Jane. I was and still am filled with gratitude and love for this woman. All that work came down to this moment.

What was I thinking? Yet the cameras didn't wait for me to have a nervous breakdown. The music started playing and I heard, "Five, four, three, two . . . "

"I'm so excited about this next hour," said Jane. "We have a new fashion brand launching today: Belle by Kim Gravel. Welcome my good friend, Kim."

I walked through the faux doors on set, and Jane started telling America about my brand and my new products.

While the red light of the live TV indicated the cameras were rolling, I knew Amy was pacing back and forth in the green room. She was watching the show live and monitoring the computer, which displayed some data: the number of purchases made online over the phone and in what sizes, how many items were left in stock, how many calls during the last ten seconds, and—one important data point—how close the segment was to meeting its goal. Other screens showed what viewers see while watching from their sofas. It's that high tech, y'all.

Amy ran back and forth to keep an eye on the sales because we had a goal to meet. No matter how much they might like my personality, if we didn't make our goal, we wouldn't make it long-term.

"And I particularly like this blouse," Jane said. "So pink! So fun!"

I smiled and laughed and pointed. I don't really remember the details of that show except I was sweating like a hog in heat. But I do remember slightly turning my head when Susan ran out onto the set and began shifting her weight from one foot to the other. What had happened? Did a fire break out in the warehouse? Was there a missile strike? Did she need to find a bathroom?

Finally, when we transitioned from one clothing item to the next, I was able to glance more fully in her direction.

That's when she gave me a thumbs-up sign. "We've met the goal!" she mouthed, like a kid in the library trying not to be heard by the librarian. "We're good! You did it!"

I exhaled in relief, joy running through every vein. As soon as the show ended, I sprinted into the control room, and everyone erupted. Cheers. Tears.

Later on when we launched Belle Beauty with just one product, it sold out.

I couldn't have done it alone. Jane, Susan, Leslie, Amy, Colleen, Siobain, and Mom. With these powerful women, I was supported and ready for more. If you have the patience, God will bring the right people. He brought me Oliver and Lifetime, and then He assembled a new team for QVC.

If you have the confidence to walk in your calling, God will bring opportunity. Keep on working and keep on believing. God doesn't just match your offering. He's a five-loaves-and-two-fishes type of guy—the best investment you can ever make (John 6:1–14). I tell you this story to dare you to dream. Dream *big* and then trust the process big. Years ago,

If you have the confidence to walk in your calling, God will bring opportunity. Keep on working and keep on believing.

I dreamed that I wanted to build my brands and be on QVC, and that opportunity found me. Your opportunity will find you! What do you desire? What things are written down on the pages of your heart? Just keep believing, preparing, and waiting; they're coming to you.

The vastness that surrounds you is small compared to the bigness inside your heart. You are a cocreator with the Most High God. Your desire to fulfill your calling is not just a lofty idea. It's a seed that's been planted in you from the beginning of time. It's big, it's vast, it's all-encompassing, and it will be fulfilled. God promises that. "Take delight in the LORD, and he will give you your heart's desires," we are told in Psalm 37:4 (NLT). And God doesn't lie.

We have real desires that we try to satisfy in various ways—through romance, career aspirations, and seeking importance. Sometimes we achieve this in life, and sometimes we don't. But in both failure and success, our deepest desires still linger, waiting for our ultimate satisfaction. True desire is not what we want or think we need. We got it wrong. We're trying to scratch an itch that we cannot reach. God knows what is best, and He hears our hearts' true desires. He will give you the desires of your heart. But it's in His time.

You will face hardships, obstacles, and maybe even a lawsuit, but that is one way you can know you're on the right path. Don't let it shake you. It's time to level up, girl! If you weren't where you're supposed to be, you wouldn't have this opposition. If God brings you to it, He'll fill you with the stamina, courage, and perseverance to get you through it. Many times, during the road to launch on QVC, I was afraid, lonely, and worried I'd miss my chance. Truth is, even if you do miss your chance, the story is not over. You wake up another day. And new opportunities await. Failure does not win.

You make decisions in your life based on the destination, not based on what is happening right now. Keep your eyes on the prize. Hold onto your vision. What God has for you is for you. Nothing will ever take that away.

Failure does not win.

If you are ready to level up, ask yourself a few questions.

Are your dreams and goals worth fighting for? I think so, big time! So put on your boxing gloves and start training to go eight rounds or until there's a knockout.

Have you been waiting a long time? Keep believing and start patiently preparing.

What can you do today to get a step closer to your vision?

There's a new level for you. Wait for it. Prepare for it. Fight for it. When your face is pressed against that dirty window of life, wondering what will happen, know that you may only be able to see through that glass, darkly . . . but soon, you'll level up, Buttercup!

10 Southern Sayings That Should Make a Comeback

1. Mess with the bull, and you're gonna get the horns.
2. If it doesn't apply, let it fly.
3. You can't make a silk purse out of a sow's ear.
4. A sharp axe is better than a big muscle.
5. No one is a stranger—just a friend you haven't met yet.

6. Once a man, twice a child.
7. Go on and cry; you will pee less.
8. If common sense was lard, no one would be able to grease a pan.
9. Never get above your raising.
10. Make sure the squeeze is worth the juice.

Ten

Don't Let Anyone Call You Out of Your Name

There is a stubbornness about me that never can bear to be frightened at the will of others. My courage always rises at every attempt to intimidate me.

—Jane Austen

"Come on, ref, are you blind?" yelled the coach.

I was sitting in the stands of my kids' school, where my seventh grader Beau played on the basketball team. I've never been a big basketball fan, but I was proud of him. He worked hard and loved the game. Our team was down by twenty points, but the boys were doing their best and giving it all they had. Being a coach of young pageant hopefuls, I knew giving your best is a win even if you are losing.

"What's wrong with y'all? Do you guys even know how to play basketball?" barked the coach to the bench full of seventh graders. I quickly looked at other parents around me to make sure I wasn't hearing things and asked a mother beside me, "What's up with this coach?"

"Oh, that's just how he is," she responded. "We've been dealing with this for years." No one seemed surprised by the coach's uncontrolled outbursts on display at this game. I just stored this experience in the red-flag folder in my mind. The game ended, we lost by twenty-eight points, and I knew it was going to be a long season.

It was Tuesday, and time for another basketball game, this time an away game. But when we went to the basketball games, the coach acted like the fate of the world rested on the outcome of any particular game. There's so much pressure now for kids to win and perform at a high level. It starts earlier and earlier as each year passes. These kids are pressured to win. They are even expected to market and promote themselves like they are on a professional level. They have to have a highlight reel, social media hype, and garner the attention of college coaches before they've hit puberty. But how could we expect our kids to train and perform like professionals, when some coaches are not coaching even at the basic level, not to mention inspiring them to be more? Shouldn't coaches be developing, guiding, and helping these players achieve growth and confidence?

I couldn't make it to the upcoming game because I was knee-deep in work deadlines. So Travis and Blanton went to

Beau's game, which our school—once again—lost. Afterward, Travis and Blanton walked out in the main lobby of the gym as they waited for Beau to come out of the locker room. When Travis heard screaming, it stopped him dead in his tracks. He looked at other people in the lobby. Everyone froze in shock and disbelief. Travis was confused.

Who was screaming? Was there something wrong?

Travis walked closer to the screaming and the words got clearer.

"You're the worst players I've ever seen! You are an embarrassment to the game of basketball. You all are losers and should never play the game again."

Sometimes, coaches in movies seem to be patterned after drill sergeants, but this was not that. He had a frantic tone that alarmed Travis. Suddenly, the door flew open, and the coach shot out and slammed the door before scurrying away, leaving a bunch of young boys sitting alone in the locker room.

At dinner that night, Travis told me the story. Beau's head was down, looking into his chicken nuggets. I'd been seeing a change in Beau. Negative self-talk. Saying, "I'm not good enough." Being old school, I'm all for coaching kids out of their comfort zone. And y'all, I'm not a "my kid is the greatest of all time" parent either. But this change wasn't the normal pimple-faced, preteen insecurity typical in a twelve-year-old boy. Beau was a different kid in less than two months. He was sheepish, withdrawn, and always held his head down in shame.

We just can't have a full-grown man talking to these kids like that, I thought. *Next game, I'm going. It might be time to move this dude from the red-flag file to now-you-ticked-off-a-mama file.*

His antics in the ensuing games shocked me even more. The next game we were down by four, with two minutes to go, when the ref called a foul. The coach flipped out, lost control, and confronted the ref.

The buzzer sounded, the game was over, and we lost. The coach stormed out, and I followed him. I spotted him as he was getting into his car, so I motioned to him that I wanted to chat. (That's southern for "confront.")

"No," he said, as soon as I asked to talk. "I can't speak to you."

Apparently, he'd made a rule that no one was allowed to talk to him until twenty-four hours after the game after a loss. What is this? The NBA? We were talking about seventh-grade kids playing a game. But I didn't know anything about this asinine rule (and at this rate, since we lost every game, I'd never get to talk to the man).

"What do you mean, I can't talk to you?" I asked.

But he drove off.

Many parents had complained to the leadership of the school, but this coach just kept getting a pass for his bad behavior. I had to think there was something bigger at play.

What was this experience trying to teach not only Beau but also me?

As a parent, I was at a loss. We had gone to the school's leadership and directly to the coach himself to address these issues. My family always taught me to face problems head-on. Don't let something fester. It wasn't fair to Beau to remove him from the team and make him quit a game he loves to play. Why punish Beau for someone else's bad behavior? I had to get my thoughts and myself in control. So before I lost my cool—two wrongs don't make a right—I needed divine intervention on how to handle this one.

But then the breaking point happened. Beau came home from practice one night; his head was held down and he didn't want to eat. And I knew if Beau wanted to skip a meal, we had an issue. He'd worked harder in order to win this guy's approval. We'd raised him to believe that when life deals you setbacks, you have to work hard. That's normally the case. But his hard work was no antidote; he was a hamster running on a wheel. Going nowhere.

"Do you want to stick it out?" I asked him.

"Yeah, Mom," he said. "I don't want to quit."

We had to do something. I don't believe in quitting when times get tough, but I do believe in strategizing how to handle the tough times.

"Beau, listen to me carefully," I said. "Don't let this coach call you out of your name."

For the first time, Beau's head popped up, hope on his face. "What do you mean by that?"

I knew he was absorbing every syllable. "When people call you names, it's really a reflection of who they are, not who you are. You have to stop and say, 'Well, who am I?' You're not a loser, so what are you?"

He shuffled in his seat.

"What does the coach call you?"

"A loser."

"Who are you really?"

He didn't answer.

"Who are you really?" I asked again.

"Beau Gravel."

"I don't see the word 'loser' in that name, do you?"

"No, ma'am."

"The next time that man says you're a loser, I want you to stand up and walk out. But before you walk out, I want you to look him in his eyes, in front of all your team, and say, 'No sir, you are the one acting like a loser.' And walk out."

"Do you want me to get suspended?"

"Whatever. I'll deal with the school," I said. "Just do what I tell you to do."

I told Beau, "You're not who others say you are. When someone tries to name you, ask yourself a question: 'Who am I really?' If you know who you are, it's like water rolling off a duck's back. The words might sting at first, and they might take you off a little bit for a minute. You might even think, 'Are they right?' But no, they're not."

Even as I said the words to Beau, I knew he'd never do it. That's not Beau. He's only selectively confrontational, meaning he's not gonna stand up to adults in authority over him, even with his mama's permission. Beau has always stood up for the little guy, but he wasn't standing up for himself. That's why I wanted to give him permission to take a stand for himself and his teammates. Wrong is wrong, even if adults are the ones doing the bullying. Though he didn't confront the coach, the conversation changed him.

The confidence that had been draining out of him began to reappear. He smiled more, walked confidently, and worked even harder. (I didn't know that was possible because he'd worked so hard already.) You could see the difference. Even the coach asked, "What's happening, Beau?" Beau changed that night. He was a different kid, and I saw hope come back as the season came to a close.

They didn't win one game all season. You never win doing that kind of junk. The coach was still yelling, being discouraging, and calling them losers. But Beau wasn't believing a word he said. I think one of the biggest fights for us in life is to fight back against the names people call us and to not let the world name you. No one can do that for you. You have to do it yourself, and Beau did.

The next season, Beau moved up to eighth grade, which meant he had a new coach who happened to be a former NBA player. This season was like night and day. It was the same boys but a different team. Each kid played his position with precision. It was a joy to watch each of these boys grow and become who they really are. They still didn't win all their games—maybe around four that season—but that wasn't the point. In my opinion, they won the championship when it came to playing as a team.

At the end of the season, under the leadership of that NBA player coach, Beau was chosen as an all-star player of the year and best defensive player. But this isn't about the vindication of my son. This is about standing up for yourself. When you stand up for yourself, you win. When you know who you are and who you are not, that's the ultimate win.

"Remember when I said not to let anybody call you out of your name?" I asked Beau recently.

"Yeah. I am Beau Gravel!"

And I thought, *Son, don't you ever forget it.*

What names have others tried to put on you? Resist those

names. Know who you are. You are a child of the Most High God. You aren't a hodgepodge mishmash of leftover scraps. You were wonderfully made to be *you.* You are wonderful; never answer to anything else.

In this book, right now, I am offering permission for you to stand up *for* yourself and stand up *to* yourself.

The good thing is no matter what anyone says about you or even what you say about yourself God always has a better word.

Negative self-talk needs to go because we talk to ourselves worse than anyone else. The tongue is described as "the pen of a ready writer" in Psalm 45:1 (KJV). That means our mouths are fast to express the thoughts overflowing from our minds. Our tongue is a scribe of what's in our hearts. So when you catch yourself talking trash about yourself, it's a signal that you need to change what's in your mind. It's time to be set free from self-rejection. Pay attention to what you call yourself. Stop being like Beau's coach calling yourself a loser because you made a mistake, had a bad thought, or didn't live up to someone else's expectations. Stop talking yourself out of success and into the ditch of "less than."

I feel convicted even as I write this, because recently I recorded myself all day talking with a small digital tape recorder. After two days, I went back and listened. To my shock, I said over one hundred hateful, negative things about myself and to myself. And here's the kicker: the things I said were untrue. The characteristics I criticized were actually some of my strengths and my superpowers. I commented that I was too loud, too boisterous, and needed to tone it down.

And that was just out loud. I had no way of recording my internal jabs at myself.

You aren't a
hodgepodge mishmash
of leftover scraps.
You were wonderfully
made to be *you.*
You are wonderful;
never answer to
anything else.

Try this yourself. Leave a recorder on for several days. It's like reality TV. You'll forget it's there and get what your verbal patterns are. You'll be surprised at what comes out of your mouth!

We are so loose with our words, but they really matter. That old saying, "Sticks and stones will break my bones, but words will never hurt me" is simply not true. I've been hurt by words more than sticks and stones. And my own words have hurt me more than the haters'. We can talk ourselves into our depression, into struggles if we aren't mindful.

I didn't want Beau to experience that. I wanted Beau to develop his own mental toughness and resilience. You think that teachers, coaches, and others give it you. But they can't. Those are gifts you have to give yourself. Stop believing what others say about you. Don't let them define you based on their perception. And by the way, check what you're saying about yourself too. Speak to yourself with respect, love, kindness, admiration, and mercy, because that's how God speaks to you. If you hear people you love saying terrible things about themselves, wouldn't you stop them? Yes. Why wouldn't God feel that way about you too?

Speak to yourself with respect, love, kindness, admiration, and mercy, because that's how God speaks to you.

Girl, today, right now. Look back in that mirror.

What are you saying to yourself?

What are you believing about yourself? "I am too ______."

Fill in the blank. (Your criticisms will be different than the ones I heap on myself.) Or, "I am always _____."

What are the names you're calling yourself?

W. C. Fields said, "It ain't what they call you; it's what you answer to!"[1]

What name do you answer to? If people demean you, then they have the problem. If people call you out of your name, it's a signal they are not confident in themselves. They are trying to find something to give themselves value. They're only trying to keep you on their basic level—misery truly does love company—but you can soar like an eagle. If someone wants to stay low, that's on them. If you stay with them down in the ravines of life, that's on you. This is a learned behavior. Stop listening to what other people say about you. This pattern of learned behavior might've started early for you (like Beau, in the seventh grade), but you can stop it.

Be careful who you keep company with. You may not be able to change the company around you, but you can be careful what you let seep into your soul. I gave Beau permission not to believe the lies. Now, I am giving *you* permission not to believe the lies of criticisms like you're too fat, you're dumb, or you're not beautiful. It might take a while to get other people to notice that you're not letting their toxicity into your life, but your internal change can be swift.

It's vital to recognize when people call you out of your name and to handle it so that it does not disrupt your pursuit of your calling.

You may be underestimated and undervalued by someone in your life. But don't let that sideline you. Don't let anyone sideline you, including yourself. Don't be your own hater. If someone tells you that you are less than, you need to have the confidence to tell them who you really are. Tell them strong enough, lest they forget. It may be that you have to work harder and smarter than what that person says. So, if you are in a tough situation at work or at home, don't let the harsh words of others get inside your spirit.

> How you think about yourself today determines who you will be tomorrow.

Don't let anyone call you out of your name. And if they do, don't believe them. Fill your mind and your mouth with the words of who you really are—blessed, brilliant, beautiful, and getting better every day.

How you think about yourself today determines who you will be tomorrow. You might be called a loser and sent to sit on the bench right now. But I bet you a dollar to a doughnut that you're on your way to being the MVP.

7 Don'ts You Must Always Do!

1. Don't neglect your soul.
2. Don't believe everything you think about yourself.
3. Don't believe everything others think about you, either.
4. Don't take yourself too seriously.
5. Don't allow momentary desires to distract you from who you're becoming.
6. Don't accept less from yourself or from others.
7. Don't wait for perfect conditions to live your life.

Eleven

Faith It Till You Make It

And will you succeed? Yes! You will, indeed! (98 and 3/4 percent guaranteed) Kid, you'll move mountains.

—Dr. Seuss

Honk, honk!

The car behind me honked when the crossing guard, in her bright orange vest, motioned for me to move up. I was in the car line at school, hoping to get the last little bit of work in before picking up the boys. I edged up the ten feet and went back to my email.

My eye landed on a message from the *Steve Harvey* show. I loved getting to be on his show and was thankful to be invited back again and again. Not only did I enjoy doing what

I love with the funniest man on the planet, I also liked the whole experience. When they reached out, I already knew I'd say yes.

"Kim, we want to have you on for a field segment," the email began. I edged up closer to the school and tried to hide my phone from the crossing guard, but I couldn't put this email down. I'd been on the show as a panelist, but never for my very own field segment. A field segment is a feature of you doing a segment or mini series by yourself. Not in studio. This would be a huge opportunity for me to show daytime television I had the skills to carry a whole segment. "We want you to be a 'confidence coach' for a single woman named Tracy who's an accomplished writer and professor but wants to learn how to date with confidence."

I didn't date a lot, but there's one thing I know about men. They love a chase; they want what they can't have. Dating's not a game, but you have to have the confidence to step into the arena. I could help this woman.

A teacher knocked on my window, and I jumped.

"Hey, Miss Kim," she said, smiling. "We ask all parents to please put down their phones in the car pickup line." I put my phone down and turned to greet Beau and Blanton, who were already crawling in the back.

I put on my cheery, happy-to-see-you voice. "How was your day—"

"I'm hungry." Beau cut me off. I swear, these kids have never been full a day in their lives. We pulled out of the school parking lot and went through McDonald's, ordering chicken nuggets but praying for their nutrition (I believe in prayer, y'all). But the whole time, I was thinking about going on the

Steve Harvey show, staying in fancy hotels, eating food I didn't have to order through a window, and did I mention no kids?

By the time I got home, I started packing, even though the show was two weeks away, and preparing the advice I'd give this woman. Everyone deserves a chance at true love, so I went to the airport and climbed into my seat on the plane. First class, baby.

"Ma'am, may I give you a hot towel?" the flight attendant asked me.

I don't know why they offer hot towels in first class, but I took it. The warmth of it didn't come close to the warmth I felt for having this opportunity. Not knowing what to do with this surprisingly hot cloth, I rubbed it all over my face and noticed, with embarrassment, that some of my makeup had smudged off onto the formerly white towel. I sheepishly handed it back to the flight attendant.

When I landed, my private car took me to a luxury hotel in the Gold Coast neighborhood close to Michigan Avenue and the Magnificent Mile in Chicago. The fall air was crisp and cool—at home in Georgia, it was so hot even in October—and autumn leaves from the very few trees popping up from the pavement blew over my shoes.

The hotel's decor was midcentury modern, with white plush couches. They looked so comfortable and enticing that I plopped down on one before realizing they were much lower than the couches back home. I rocked back and forth to get some momentum, and I finally got up and started walking around the huge public areas.

"Would you like some champagne?" A man in a black coat held out a silver tray filled with flutes of sparkling liquid.

Was this free? But I was afraid to take one, because I was high already about doing the show.

When the bellboy took my bags—mine was Samsonite, compared to the other guests' Louis Vuittons—I was country come to town! I rummaged through my purse, hoping to have at least ten dollars to tip him. I never carry cash. But I didn't want to have a reputation of being cheap like my husband.

The hotel had one of Chicago's most fashionable restaurants, where gorgeous people sipped cocktails and drank draft beer. Before I went to my room, I ducked into the restaurant just to people-watch. Since I'm from a small town in Georgia, I rarely get to just sit and relax to observe the unique cast of characters only witnessed in the wild in urban spaces.

I watched as ostentatiously wealthy people elegantly chatted, their wrists dripping with diamonds and platinum. Even the men were decked out with suits and shoes—you can always tell ooh-la-la people by their shoes. It was better than *National Geographic*! If I watched long enough, I bet I'd see some mating rituals, but I needed to focus on the show.

I ordered from the farm-to-table menu—the appetizers were twenty-five dollars!—and ate shrimp from whatever world-renowned chef was behind the scenes (better than my typical ham and cheese) and googled Tracy to see what I was dealing with. I found her blog about "Doomed Dating" on the *Huffington Post,* where she'd been chronicling her run of bad dates. She struggled with knowing if she revealed too much emotional baggage too soon to some dates. With others, she held back and was never able to achieve the right amount of interest. I could tell she had not learned the delicate art of flirting.

I couldn't wait to give my dating advice to this woman, especially since Amy never listens to me. I was going to do a series during which Tracy would go out on dates. I could tell from her thumbnail photo on her blog that she was beautiful and clearly intelligent, but she just needed a little extra *oomph.*

The next morning, my driver took me to the underground dropoff at NBC Studios, and I felt like a movie star. I regretted leaving my sunglasses because it was that kind of moment. I knew every other panelist had some sort of specialty like being a fitness coach, psychologist, or stylist to the stars. And some part of me—like 15 percent of me—felt a little out of my depth. Steve thought I was worthy of time on his national platform just because I was me. I ignored the niggling 15 percent of insecurity and sank into the 85 percent of me that was ebullient about being there.

"Thank you so much," I said to the driver in my friendliest and most apologetic southern accent. I dug in my purse, but I didn't have any extra cash after giving it all to the bellboy. "I'll catch ya next time." Now, along with the stress of the show, I had the stress of finding an ATM.

I walked to my dressing room, where Jason, the show's makeup artist, was waiting for me.

"Hey, girl! How's my Georgia peach?" He was from Hotlanta too, and he leaned in to hug me. "I'm always happy to see you, because that means I get a day off." He eyed my hot pink Caboodle makeup case and placed it on the counter for me.

"Don't take it personally," I said to him as I started unpacking my bag and placing tubes of lipstick and bobby pins and duct tape on the dressing room counter. Why did I have duct tape? To get the perfect cleavage and shave a few inches off your bust line, you tape your tatas together. I was using this old pageant trick so the cameramen wouldn't have to use a wide-angle lens.

"I know. All women have their bag full of goodies." He picked up my eyeliner and nodded approvingly. "And every pageant girl wants to do it herself."

He was right. I could have been stranded in the Amazon and lived for three months out of that Caboodle. I'd brought snacks, crackers, granola bars, some chewing gum, a bottle of water, and every shade of lip gloss. I got dressed and did my makeup and felt expectant as I waited for my cue and listened backstage.

Steve announced to the audience and to America that he was gonna help Tracy find her man. First, he explained, the show worked on her outside. Lawrence Zarian, a fashion expert in the television industry, gave this woman—who had yet to be revealed—a head-to-toe makeover with the Steve Harvey glam squad. She got her hair extensions, lowlights, and conditioner that made her look amazing. To accentuate her green eyes, Lawrence added lashes. Lastly, he gave her a cute blue dress and some thigh-high boots.

Steve put her "before" photo up. She looked sort of plain, with jeans and a pullover. Then he called for her to come on out and show her new self. When she came out, she was the new glamorous person Lawrence had promised.

I listened as Lawrence explained all he had done to achieve this new look.

"Part one is done," said Steve. "Now it's time for the next step: a confidence lesson." Steve explained Tracy needed more self-assurance. "For that, I brought in another pro."

That was my cue. I felt beautiful, confident, and ready for the adrenaline rush of a live studio audience. Not many people get to be a recurring guest on a hit show. In that moment, I felt like I was something special.

The joy of that experience rushed through me as I burst forward through open doors onto the sound stage. The audience clapped for little ole me from Lilburn, Georgia, with its railroad that runs straight through it with trains every hour. And there I was, on a national television stage greeted by the sound of hundreds of people clapping.

Steve and Lawrence were sitting on stools on one side of the stage, and Tracy was standing—in her cute blue dress—at the front. I was wearing a black dress and high heels, and I strode through those doors, head held high.

Steve looked at me and said, "She has more confidence than any woman I've ever met." Speaking about me. The audience applauded.

But my heart sank. If he had complimented me on anything else—my pageant skills, my television show, my life coaching—I would've been fine. But when he complimented me on my confidence, right there in front of America, I questioned my confidence and competence and the doubt crept in. The applause in real life swelled as I walked out on stage and saw Tracy. But it subsided in my soul, replaced by the voice of my inner critic.

Who are you to talk to anybody about confidence? You're ridiculous, Kim. You've got on Spanx and a Miraclesuit girdle at the same time, and you're telling this educated woman—who's an author—how to live her life with confidence? And you're doing this in front of a stylist for the stars? Who are you? You've never done anything. You're not enough.

The above internal conversation happened in a fraction of a second. That seems implausible, but I can go down a rabbit hole faster than Alice in Wonderland. The audience was still applauding, but I was already falling. Yet the cameras still rolled, and everyone was looking to me for a confidence lesson, and maybe you are too.

The thing about confidence is that it is not always consistent. Sometimes, when we need it the most, it's like we're playing Marco Polo in our head.

Here's how *that* one played out.

The show had to go on, though I was suddenly the least confident "confidence coach" in the history of television. I was devastated, embarrassed, and felt out of my league. But I wasn't gonna let anyone else know that.

Absent a feeling of total confidence, I performed it. When Steve complimented me on my confidence, I stuck one hand on my hip, threw the other hand in the air, and gave Steve a high five.

"All right," I said. I looked like a character out of a movie, full of bravado and ease.

Then, I—somehow with a straight face—told Tracy I could bring out the confidence in her and change her approach to dating.

"If we can put a man on the moon," I said, "Steve Harvey can put a man on you."

I managed to help Tracy, but I was preaching to the choir.

I had a head knowledge of confidence, but the soul knowledge was hiding.

In fact, it was life changing for Tracy and me.

For the rest of the show, I put on my confidence like armor. And later, when I was scrolling through Twitter, I read something that stopped me in my tracks. Social media is funny. People say and ask the craziest things. "Kim, I just love you" or "Kim, where did you get those earrings?" I've even had several men ask for pictures of my feet. Weird, right? But I kept scrolling, and one particular tweet made me pause.

"What does this lady know about confidence? She seems insecure to me," a man wrote. Reading this tweet made me acknowledge there was some truth there—he was onto something. Normally, I don't respond to negativity on social media. But after some real thought, I responded to this gentleman in four simple words: "Sir, you are right." I have insecurities; don't we all?

We think being insecure is a bad thing, but it doesn't have to hold us back. It's a reminder that we are human and need something bigger than ourselves to be truly confident. Insecurities don't stop us. We need to stop wasting time trying to get rid of insecurities, because we're just majoring on the minors. Our insecurities do not outweigh our greatness, and they will come and go; but your calling, like God, will never leave you even if at times it feels like it.

Beau accidentally taught me a lesson about this. He had a world geography project that was very confusing. On the one hand, the students were told in class to write about a crisis or pandemic either past or present that affected the population, but Beau missed that day of class, so his teacher told him to

Our insecurities do not outweigh our greatness, and they will come and go; but your calling, like God, will never leave you even if at times it feels like it.

refer to the online curriculum. This instruction was to write about a *chronic* disease that affected the population, either past or present. In writing his assignment, Beau figured out that there was a discrepancy. One directive called it a *crisis* or pandemic and the other a *chronic* disease. In talking with me, Beau pointed out that they are two different things.

"Mom, chronic diseases go on and on, but a crisis or pandemic only lasts for a short period of time." He began chomping down on his sour cream and onion potato chips. It was a Psalm 8:2 moment for me ("Out of the mouth of babes . . . hast thou ordained strength" KJV), because his comment struck me to the core.

It blew my mind. I'd been treating my "crisis of confidence" as a chronic condition. And if you are anything like me, you have too! But your lack of confidence is not chronic. It's a short crisis, but this too shall pass.

So when you are feeling that pang of insecurity, don't run from it. Recognize it, acknowledge it, and accept it. Heck, maybe even love it. Because it's what makes you human, it's what makes you *you*. I'm sharing on these pages the truth of what I feel, what I struggle with, and what I am.

Here's one that came at me fast. In the beginning of the COVID-19 pandemic, I had just finished my show on QVC. I got the last plane from Pennsylvania, where their headquarters was, back to Georgia. There were six people on that plane, and we barely got near one another. Fear was in the air. Uncertainty. QVC would have to learn to do its business in a different way. I would have to do my business a different way. Like so many others, I had to pivot. I had to build a studio in my home and learn how to broadcast and connect with the QVC hosts. All the while I was now homeschooling my boys. I didn't know if it could be done. And I had just turned fifty. Let me tell you, girl, that is a big birthday.

It all shook me to my foundation. So many people depended on me. I wanted to give up. I didn't know how to move forward. I was depressed, and I lay in bed for days. Sometimes you don't do things until you have to do them. Let's be honest, we don't have the luxury of sitting around being depressed. We march on. That's what we women do. I didn't know how I could keep up doing my show, my business, my life.

After that big birthday, I had to decide to do some heavy lifting with my trusted faith muscles. Talk about muscle memory. I would say to myself, "I'm not sure how this will work out, but it will all be okay." We were all saying that during this unknown time. I decided to do something new, to start small again. I leaned into my calling—"To edify." I knew other people, particularly women, were also going through a lot, also maybe having a crisis of confidence. I wanted to laugh out loud, bring joy, connect with other women who were in the same boat, and share the little bit of stuff I've learned. I knew that I would also receive that back from them. So I started my podcast, *The Kim Gravel Show,* which gave me a whole new way to share in the community of women.

Turns out that I was not as alone as I had felt I was. Now, through my podcast, I get to build relationships with women all over the world who deal with the same insecurities, fears, and doubts that I do. Because together, us regular folk are powerful. There are people who set out to be wise, who study theology, psychology, and so on. Then there are people who become wise through living, through experience, and by collecting confidence over time like my parents, the Nancys, and my grandma.

I'm tired of wearing a mask and pretending everything is okay. I'm even tired of pretending I have it all together—that I can do a show, write a book, pay the light bill, and find the right eyeliner to make my eyes pop all before making it home in time to have a well-balanced meal on the table. Or let's face it, run through the drive-through.

It's okay to feel "not enough," ill at ease, and insecure in this life, just like I do. Insecurities don't mess you up; they make you up. They are part of who you are. Getting rid of them would be like leaving the salt off your potato chips. Share that flavor with your friends, family, and even yourself. It's the stuff that truly connects with people, and that's how we shore each other up. We are flawed, insecure, and sometimes a little salty but full of flavor. Let's face it, we all would be bored if we were flawless. So I say own your crises of confidence, however cumbersome they may be.

Insecurities don't mess you up; they make you up.

Others say, "Fake it till you make it," but I say let's quit faking it. Let's "faith it till we make it," because faith has substance and is real. When you have faith, you know that this too shall pass—you can weather the crisis. It is not chronic.

In a crisis we need encouragement, community, and connection. By now, I feel like we are friends and have made a connection. You've come all the way through these pages, and I feel like—you and me—we've bonded. Do you feel it? Whenever you feel insecure, have a crisis of confidence, or feel like you are faking it to the world, girl, just remember you are in good company.

10 Tips to Collect Your Confidence

KIM GRAVEL

1. Keep the faith in the face of setbacks, and you'll see your confidence shape up real fast.
2. Surround yourself with people you can learn from.
3. Have daily nonnegotiables. Be sure to schedule them.
4. Say yes to opportunities that intimidate or scare you.
5. Don't get ahead of yourself.
6. Don't make a decision when you're confused.
7. Only look back to measure how far you have come.
8. Aim to achieve small, bite-size accomplishments every day.
9. Walk through open doors of opportunity.
10. When you start having feelings of insecurity, acknowledge them, embrace them, and share them with others.

Twelve

Fashioned for Greatness

> *"The young are not afraid of telling the truth."*
>
> —*Anne Frank*

Arcado Elementary School in Liburn, Georgia, had a gigantic oak tree in the front, a fence keeping the kids out of the cow pasture behind the school, and an annual talent show I wanted to win.

As soon as my teacher announced the upcoming contest, I looked at five of my girlfriends at recess. "Who wants to be in an air band?"

Their little heads nodded in enthusiasm, and I knew I had my squad. I was only in the fifth grade, but I wanted to take first prize.

"What's an air band?" my friend asked hesitantly.

"It's when you pretend to play musical instruments to recorded music," I said. "But you don't have to know how to play anything. I'll sing live, but you guys can just pretend."

I named our group Rare Edition. We didn't have to play any instruments, but we did have to look the part.

I set to work.

First, I made every piece of clothing we would wear on talent show day—I bought baseball shirts that were white in the middle with long purple sleeves. I bought iridescent iron-on letters and spelled out "Rare Edition" across the chest. I asked the girls to wear their best jeans. Some of them had Jordache or Gloria Vanderbilt jeans.

All that was for the band. I needed something special, because I was going to sing live—actually sing, instead of pulling a Milli Vanilli—so I made myself a purple blouse to go with a pair of pants and sewed a purple racing stripe down each leg.

Then I found the music. At the time, I was obsessed with the movie *Xanadu* and Olivia Newton-John, may she rest in peace. I had the *Xanadu* soundtrack record, which had an instrumental version of "Suspended in Time" on the B side. (For you young'uns, the B side is the flip side of a vinyl record that typically receives less attention. A record is a large, round . . . oh, never mind.)

Then I borrowed the instruments I needed to assemble a legit air band. I got an entire drum set, a bass guitar, a rhythm guitar, and a keyboard. Since I couldn't drive, I had to get Mom to take me to a friend's house, where I loaded up the big, clunky pieces.

I put my parents through the ringer. My mom says I was

a hard kid to raise because I always had something going on and dragged her around to help me. (And I'm still dragging her around!) Mom took me to rehearsals, dropped me off, and came back a few hours later. She wasn't a stage mom. She has never been a stage mom.

Just think about how much effort I, as a flat-chested, scrawny ten-year-old little girl, put into this fifth-grade talent show. Wow! Sitting here writing this I'm reminded how lucky I was back then. I could dream without interruption and create without comparison. Back then, we couldn't Amazon Prime a package to our house in two days. So I had to plan everything, from the smallest details like the iron-on patches to the biggest like the entire drum set I needed onstage. But none of it was difficult. It all just came naturally to me.

When you were young, what came naturally to you? Stop and really think about that question and then write down what you remember. What did you do with confidence? Are you still doing any of those things today? If not, why not?

When you were young, what came naturally to you?

On the day of the talent show, I was ready for my moment. I was wearing my purple blouse, racing-stripe pants, and a headband to keep my mullet looking good. (Billy Ray Cyrus stole my look!) My all-girl air band was ready to pretend they were the next The Go-Go's. The Arcado Elementary lunchroom was absolutely packed with students, faculty, and parents. There were no seats left in that school cafeteria. The audience was filled with adults—all those big butts in those child-size cafeteria chairs. It was so packed that people were sitting on the ice cream coolers in the back. You couldn't get one more body in that cafeteria.

We were the final act. I waited and clapped politely at the other talents onstage. When they called the name Rare Edition, we set up the instruments and the air band assumed their positions. I stood in front. The instrumental version of the song "Suspended in Time" began to play, and I closed my eyes for a minute and imagined myself as Olivia Newton-John belting out the lyrics.

I started to sing, and I sang with all the force I had in my little body.

I bet there's never been a more heartfelt talent show entry than that one in the cafeteria that day. When we finished, the lunchroom erupted in applause. I bowed and bowed again and stood there and soaked it in. A few minutes later, when the judges made their decision, Rare Edition had won first place.

Memories are weird. They pop up when you least expect them and sometimes penetrate you to the core. That's what happened as I wrote this book. I looked at my life, and I thought, *How on earth did I wind up here*? Then one night as I sat in the silence of my house—the boys and Travis were mercifully asleep—I remembered this talent show. That's when it dawned on me that every aspect of my current life and occupational trajectory could be seen in my Rare Edition experience.

I never imagined I'd make designer clothes, but looking back, I've been doing it all my life. I've been fashioning things forever. I made curtains for my bedroom as a child. I made my own swimsuit for Miss Georgia. I took old things, pillows, and other items and turned them into something else. I used to love going into the junkyard to look at all the discarded treasures that mattered to someone. I never saw myself singing professionally, but I've been singing my whole life. I never imagined I'd put together events, but I've been doing it my whole life. I've always been an entrepreneur, a self-starter. I've been self-starting stuff my entire life.

It was so natural to me that I didn't even recognize what I was doing. When things come easily to us, we sometimes take them for granted. We take our greatness for granted, but quite frequently it's all there in plain sight. *Why didn't I see it? Why do I find it surprising?*

"We can't predict the future, but we can read the patterns of the past to see how God has marked us for his purposes. He uses the past to open our future," wrote Dr. Dan Allender, a prominent Christian therapist, author, professor, and speaker. "Listen to your stories. They reveal a pattern of roles that you've played throughout your life. Without question there will be discrepancies and mind-boggling contradictions. There is evolution and transformation, but the being that a person was at age 3 still has some overlap with the inner world of that same person at age 93."[1]

In other words, your life tells a story about your calling.

Your life tells a story about your calling.

I can trace everything—the fashion line, the singing career, and my desire to entertain—back to that fifth-grade talent show. That was the launch, the kickoff.

Now I'm beginning to see and understand the stories and patterns of my life, and I see them as one big, beautiful quilted story made up of where I am now. But life also has space for the stories that are yet to come. I never thought I would be where

I am today, but I'm realizing that every decade of my life I've done something that's led me to this very moment, as I sit on my couch right now writing this book. I've been collecting confidence for this moment my whole life. I didn't go to school for it, but I went to the school of life. I didn't know that I would be a designer, make beauty products, or write this book. I didn't know these things would make my heart sing, but they do.

So let's talk about you, girl. What are you waiting for?

Everything in your life is threaded together like a beautifully designed, one-of-a-kind masterpiece.

Come and sit with me on my couch, and let's remember who you are. I'll push the throw pillows aside and make room. What do you dream of? What is your next big adventure? And here's the ultimate question: How do you discover it?

Remember a time when you did something—not for money, not to be perfect, not for validation, but just because you *loved* to do it. When you loved to sing or write or had tea parties for your stuffed animals. When you expressed your true self and not what you thought others wanted. It is that memory, in that joyous activity, that you will discover and recover your calling. We have to preserve it, protect it, guard it. The world wants to distract you with other projects, with busyness, obligations, and with scrolling on your phone.

In all the busyness and responsibilities of womanhood—caretaking, parenting, partnering, working—we can forget what it's like to have dreams for our own futures.

But if you hush and think for a moment, you can remember. Let's go back to an earlier time.

Let's imagine the little girl you were. What did she just *love* to do?

KIM GRAVEL

You've been collecting confidence your whole life through the experiences you've lived.

What did she dream about?

What made her feel alive?

What did she do that came easy to her? (Drawing, baking, organizing?)

If you're not still doing those things, why did you give it up to do something else?

What gave you joy? (For me, it is still Pepperidge Farms coconut cake. I buy that cake because my kids won't eat it!)

You may have had a hard childhood that shaped you. You may have been marginalized. You may have been held back. But trust me, you've had a Rare Edition moment that you've forgotten about, a moment when your calling peeked through. You've grown older, time has worn on you, and life may have beaten you down. But the calling God has for you will lift you up if you let it. He put that calling in you when you were in your mother's womb because He fashioned you for greatness. It's right there in Psalm 139:13–14: "For you fashioned my inmost being, you knit me together in my mother's womb. I thank you because I am awesomely made, wonderfully; your works are wonders—I know this very well" (CJB).

Most people focus on the stuff that matters least.

Are you stuck trying to turn yourself into a pretzel doing things that you think you should do and not what makes your heart sing? It's time to take the most of what you have and make something of it.

At this moment, I want you to drill down to find this "fearfully and wonderfully made" person holding this book—*you*! Think about what puts you in a happy place. Let's gather up your stories and stitch them together until the real you becomes as evident as paisley on a plaid background. Quit giving yourself away! Quit giving your talents, energy, and time to things that matter the least. Quit giving your talents, energy, and time to things that don't come naturally to you.

It's time to draw water from the well of your life and take a long, satisfying drink. You don't have to buy it, create it, look to someone else for it—your calling is already there inside of you. When you let go of all that busyness, you'll feel relieved! When you figure it out, you'll experience euphoria.

These days we talk a great deal about not being able to remember things: *Where did I put my keys? Why do I call my sons each other's names when I'm fussing at them? How did I forget that fourth Zoom call of the day?* But I'm asking you to focus now on remembering.

Frederick Buechner wrote, "The time is ripe for looking back over the day, the week, the year, and trying to figure out where we have come from and where we are going to, for sifting through the things we have done and the things we have left undone for a clue to who we are and who, for better or worse, we are becoming."[2]

But again and again, we avoid the long thoughts. We cling to the present out of wariness of the past. And why not, after all? We get confused. We need to escape as often as we can. Unfortunately, the escape, while it lasts, is good but short-lived. Soon, if we are not careful, we just live each day for the escape.

For instance, I work all day, feed my family, run the kids up and down to practices, and on the inside, I'm thinking *I have three more hours until I can come home and turn on* the Great British Baking Show *or* Real Housewives of Wherever, *and grab a Coke Zero and a handful of chocolates.* It's not that you shouldn't enjoy your reality TV or your handful of chocolates or your beverage of choice. All of this is a way of unwinding. But it's when we are looking forward to that and nothing else, we begin to feel empty. It doesn't really fill you up, and if you're not careful, your escape becomes your calling. When you live your life just doing what you gotta do, instead of what you were made to do, life feels like monotony instead of an adventure.

"But there is a deeper need yet," Buechner continued. "That is the need—not all the time, surely, but from time to time—to enter that still room within us all where the past lives on as a part of the present, where the dead are alive again, where we are most alive ourselves to the long journeys of our lives with all their twistings and turnings and to where our journeys have brought us. The name of the room is Remember—the room where with patience, with charity, with quietness of heart, we remember consciously to remember the lives we have lived."[3]

You can discover your calling in your youth but forget it in the trauma of growing up.

That's what I'm asking you to do. But not only am I asking you to remember the life you have lived, I'm asking you to reflect on how the moments of your life can inform your life going forward.

You can discover your calling in your youth but forget it in the trauma of growing up. Your youth is when you dreamed with no limitation, no hesitation, but only with anticipation of what could be possible for your life. That's when your calling was clear. Remember that?

Now is the time to get your air band together and to live out the big life God has planned for you. You've now collected the confidence to be who you are. Look around at the opportunities and then explore them. It's not too late. You can do this right now. Just take one step. Then take another step.

God has been prompting you toward your calling your whole life.

It's not hard; we make it hard. You've been collecting confidence your whole life through the experiences you've lived. You've failed and gotten back up. Maybe you've been married twenty-plus years and you're still together. Or you're on the other side of the divorce you never thought you would get over. Maybe you've given birth and raised teenagers who are now the prodigal sons. Or you've been a caretaker of a family member who is dying of cancer, or maybe you've overcome cancer yourself.

You have the confidence inside of you, right now, to live the life of calling you were created for. It's not something you do; it's something you've already done. You've done it countless times when you were just doing the thing that came naturally.

As we get older, things tend to fade, not to mention sag, wrinkle, get blurry, and take a different shape altogether. It's time to dream in the vivid colors we did when we were young.

God is a God of dreams. He is invested in your enjoyment. (Why else would He make puppies, Twinkies, the "Add to Cart" button, and facials?) Y'all, we are allowed to have *joy*!

God doesn't give up on us or our calling. He doesn't change His mind.

God created us to be just who we are. Don't let the screams of the world, or the whispers of your failures and shame, shape your outlook. It's time to speak faith, the language of God. Remember what Hebrews 11:1 says: "Faith is the substance [the real physical matter of which a person or thing consists and which has a tangible, solid presence] of things hoped for" (my paraphrase). What are the tangible things you are hoping for? When I was in the fifth grade, hope came to me easily as I planned my Arcado Elementary talent show debut.

> Don't let the screams of the world, or the whispers of your failures and shame, shape your outlook.

But as the years have passed, sometimes it's been harder to exist just on hope. Sometimes I have to keep reminding myself that there's more to this daily life than just the grind. I have to honor that ten-year-old in the school cafeteria who is still dreaming, creating, and singing inside of me.

What makes your soul sing? Whatever it is, it may not pay a lot or be what the world says is prestigious. You may not win a trophy in a talent show for doing the thing that makes your soul sing. But when you get in tune with what makes you content and know, *really know*, who you are, you'll be filled with hope. Be open to seeing what this is for you.

How? Here are some daily practices I use that have helped me:

- Think about the deepest dreams you used to dream about (like I used to dream about being on TV). If it's not outrageous or ridiculous, keep going. Don't take a small bite of the elephant. Bite a big chunk off! Write it down.

- Dream for yourself as you might do for others. You want the best for others, so desire the best for yourself too! Let's face it. It's easy to dream big for others. Most of us have huge hopes for our children. Why do we dream big for others and not for ourselves?
- Don't give up. Don't think about what you don't have (money, time, opportunities, etc.) that's preventing your dream from becoming a reality. Your calling will come alongside you when you take that first step forward.
- Don't feel guilty that you want too much or that you don't deserve it. You are being hopeful, and honey, you were created for this and more.

Isn't it funny that the older we get, the more we remember the good old days? When I talk to my parents or friends, we always end up talking about when we were kids, how we would run wild and free. How getting a new Pat Benatar record or watching MTV videos on TV for the first time opened our eyes to dreaming even bigger?

I have a theory about that. When we were young, we were free to be truthful with ourselves. I think it's because that's when we believed in ourselves the most. When we were younger, we would swing from vines into the creeks and didn't flinch at mosquitos or snakes. We rode bicycles down dirt paths, hitting the occasional rocks, but picking ourselves back up and going ahead anyway. We fearlessly dreamed and carelessly hoped. This was before we cared about being thin and attractive or thought about responsibilities. Back when we were whole and unafraid, when the magic of life was real and obtainable. There were no limitations on our imaginations or dreams. And we weren't afraid of saying them out loud. We didn't worry about how something was going to happen; we just did it. We didn't care how we sounded; we just knew somehow that the songs we sang into our hairbrushes while looking in our bedroom mirrors were important . . . and we knew in our bones we were important too.

Sometimes you need to look back before you can surge ahead. Let's stand in awe of our lives again and celebrate how far we've come and look forward to what's ahead. Go into that deep place and remember who you were. Remind yourself you were fashioned for greatness even before you drew your first breath.

> Remind yourself you were fashioned for greatness even before you drew your first breath.

It's time to put on your Gloria Vanderbilts—or, for you thrifty girls, those Gitanos—and harken back to being wild and free.

Because, girl, you are a *rare edition*!

You are nowhere finished with what you've started. You have a voice and a reason for being on this earth at this time, girl. If you believe this, then you'll experience more than you ever dreamed possible. You aren't just blindly going from one place to another; you are heading to a specified, beautiful place God has prepared for you in advance. And even when the world doesn't notice all you do, God does.

In a world that reduces us to various family roles—wife,

mother, daughter, grandmother, sister, aunt—always remember your most important family connection is none of these. It's that you are a child of the Most High God.

So whether you're wearing control-top pantyhose, high heels, or last week's yoga pants you still haven't washed, you're not alone, you're important, and you're special. You have everything inside you need. You've collected all the confidence you need. You've been collecting it all your life. A foundation has been laid—mentors, family, past experiences, and even your biggest mistakes. That beautiful tapestry has been fashioned with the hardship of births, deaths, friendships, breakups, and divorces. Everything you've experienced makes you who you are meant to be. Nothing was an accident; nothing was wasted. It's been poured into you from your beginning. Before you were a twinkle in your mother's eye, God had a calling for you.

We, as women, have been created for such a time as this. You are valuable, and we need you. Your kids, your husband, your family, your community—we need you walking in your calling.

Now's the time. Part one is done. Now it's time for the next step. Think back to what was true to you as a child, and now start where you are. You can do this. A crisis will pass, but confidence remains. Your glory days are always ahead.

This book is a reminder to remember who you are. You may doubt you are enough, but believe me, you are.

It's time for you to take the next step into your calling. And, girl, it's a big one. Start where you are now to become who you're meant to be.

I love you. I believe in you. You got this.

Walk boldly in your collected confidence!

Favorite Thing

There's not a moment His eye's not on you
There's not a thought you have He doesn't know
There's not a whisper spoken too softly
Oh, come hide under His wing and you'll know
He calls you Beloved, come with me

He woos you, pursues you, He chooses you
He wants you, He sees you, the real you
You are His favorite thing

He will rejoice over you with singing
He will quiet you with His love
He will delight in your very presence
Oh, come and taste, see that He's good
He calls you Beloved, come with me
He woos you, pursues you, He chooses you
He wants you, He sees you, the real you
You are His favorite thing

He calls you Beloved, come with me
He woos you, pursues you, He chooses you
He wants you, He sees you, the real you
He woos you, pursues you, He chooses you
He wants you, He sees you, the real you
You are His favorite thing

Written by Kim Gravel and Amy Goins for Beloved
Based on Zephaniah 3:17

kimisms

/ˈkim izəm/ *noun*

words of encouragement from Kim Gravel that build up and edify women and remind them to stop struggling, embrace the beauty of who they are, and step into their power and purpose.

1. This world is broken, but you aren't.
2. Fear is your frenemy. Whatever scares you can drive you toward a deeper faith if you let it.
3. God's making room for what's next. Don't be afraid to lose what you have now.
4. Stop letting minor people have major roles in your life.
5. Seek to make mistakes. The more mistakes you make, the closer you are to getting it right.
6. You can't drum up joy. You gotta call it forth from within.
7. There's gold in people; dig for it.
8. If you've never been down, how are you gonna get up?
9. To plant seeds of greatness, you gotta dig in the dirt.
10. Parenting is not what you do or say but who you are.
11. It ain't bragging if you can back it up.
12. Life doesn't have a remote control. You gotta get up and change the channel yourself.

Discussion Guide

Hope you've enjoyed this book. These questions are designed to help you or your book group go deeper.

Love you, girl. You got this!

xoxo Kim

INTRODUCTION: WHY I WROTE THIS BOOK

1. When has life knocked the breath out of you?
2. In the past, where have you turned to look for answers for the struggles you are experiencing?
3. How have you viewed yourself in the past?
4. What do you think it means to be a person of confidence?
5. Do you feel confident at this point in your life? Why or why not?
6. How does it make you feel to know that you aren't broken?

CHAPTER 1: YOUR LIFE IS EVERYTHING YOU NEVER THOUGHT BUT ALWAYS WANTED

1. Who has inspired you to find your calling, and how have they done so?

2. Have you ever compromised who you are in order to please others? Why or why not?

3. In what ways can our struggles make us stronger?

4. How does it make you feel to know that you are "fearfully and wonderfully made" (Psalm 139:14)?

5. What unique traits and features did God give you?

CHAPTER 2: IF YOU AIN'T DEAD, YOU AIN'T DONE!

1. What are some important choices that you made as a young adult, and how have those choices shaped who you are now?

2. What are some struggles you've faced that brought you closer to God? How did they do so?

3. What is the difference between a career and vocation?

4. What is a calling, and why is it important to know that we each have one?

5. What do you think God might be calling you to do at this season in your life?

6. What resonates with you about "The Calling Credo" on page 39, and why?

CHAPTER 3: DON'T EDIT YOUR STORY

1. Have you ever felt compelled to step out of your comfort zone? If so, please describe your experience.

2. In what ways are faith and belief different?

3. What do you think it looks like to trust God completely?

4. Looking back, how can you "connect some dots" about how God has worked in your life?

Which part of your life might need a bit of a shake-up?

What decisions have boosted your confidence?

What are some reasons we might not want to step out of our comfort zones?

Why do you think it's important that we not despise ourselves?

CHAPTER 4: NEVER PUT YOURSELF ON SALE

1. Why do you think we often tend to "dumb ourselves down"?

2. Why do you think we often confuse humility with self-loathing?

3. What do you think it means to "know your worth"?

4. What is something that activates you or aggravates you right now? What steps toward growth might those feelings prompt you to take?

5. What do you think the author means when she says, "Sometimes you have to be willing to lose something to gain it"?

6. What is "imposter syndrome"? Is that something you've experienced? If so, please describe your experience.

7. What are your strengths?

8. What important lessons have you learned from real-world experience?

CHAPTER 5:
LIFE IS LIKE A JELLY DOUGHNUT

1. In what ways have you changed as you've aged?

2. Why do you think it is sometimes difficult for us to embrace the changes we go through as we get older?

3. How does it make you feel to know that God fashioned you for greatness?

4. When have you felt free and exuberant?

5. Why do you think walking in our calling can bring us joy?

6. In what ways can our failures become our successes?

CHAPTER 6: I'M NOT A FAT GIRL

1. How would you describe motherhood?

2. In what ways is motherhood confusing?

3. Why is it important to know that your circumstances don't dictate who you are?

4. What are some "I am" statements you often say about yourself? In what ways are those lies?

5. What truths from God can you memorize to help you counter negative self-talk?

6. Do you agree that we often "fear loss when we have everything to gain"? Why or why not?

7. What dreams have you stopped pursuing, and why? Do you think you should pursue them again? Why or why not?

CHAPTER 7: THE MESS IS THE MESSAGE

1. When is a time God provided you with comfort and strength?

2. Have you ever felt God's presence fully? If so, what was your experience?

3. Why is it important to know that God is in control of everything?

4. What does it mean that God is omnipresent, omniscient, and omnipotent?

5. How do you need God's help now?

CHAPTER 8: ALL-YOU-CAN-EAT BUFFET

1. When you think of God's power and presence, do you feel empowered or puny? Why?

2. What is the "crumb mentality," and why do you think we experience it?

3. When have you felt comfortable being real and authentic?

4. What do you think the author means when she writes, "Calling does not equal perfection"?

5. When have you felt fulfilled?

6. What is the "why" behind your dream?

7. How do you define *beauty*?

8. If you were to write a mission statement about your calling, what do you think it would say?

CHAPTER 9: LEVEL UP, BUTTERCUP!

1. What is "power waiting"?
2. How difficult is it for you to "power wait"? What will you do to get better at it?
3. In what ways does "power waiting" develop confidence?
4. Why is it important to surround yourself with people who will support you?
5. What do you think it looks like to be your own advocate?
6. In what ways have your adversaries helped you grow and improve?

CHAPTER 10: DON'T LET ANYONE CALL YOU OUT OF YOUR NAME

1. When has someone tried to call you out of your name? How did it make you feel?

2. Do you engage in negative self-talk? Why or why not?

3. Why do you think we often "talk to ourselves worse than anyone else"?

4. Why do you think words are so powerful?

5. How does your view of yourself change when you think of being God's precious, beloved child?

CHAPTER 11: FAITH IT TILL YOU MAKE IT

1. What are your insecurities?

2. Why is it important to admit that we all have insecurities?

3. Have you ever faked confidence? If so, why, and what was the result?

4. Why do you think confidence comes and goes?

5. In what ways is a crisis different from something that is chronic?

CHAPTER 12: FASHIONED FOR GREATNESS

1. What came naturally to you when you were young?
2. What is something you love to do? How often do you get to do it?
3. What are some things you do because you think you should do them?
4. Why is it important to look at our past when pursuing our calling?
5. Do you feel as though your life is more monotonous or adventurous, and why?
6. What will your next step be in order to follow your calling?

Gratitude

Travis: Many years ago, when you tried to kiss me in the parking lot of that Mexican restaurant, did you think we'd be where we are today? Since then, I've been so grateful (over and over!) for what only God could dream up: you—a man of few words who would be the perfect match for a talker like me. Thank you for being my rock, my soulmate, my advisor. Your love and unconditional support made this book—and everything else—possible. I love you, and I could not have undertaken this journey without your support.

Beau and Blanton: When you boys showed up in this world, you changed my life. Not only did you make me a mother, you helped me to see the wonder in the world. God made you both so special and full of surprises—you keep me on my toes. I'm so blessed to have a front-row seat to your lives and can't wait to see what God has in store for you. I know it's gonna be good! I love you both to infinity and beyond!

Mom and Dad: You guys knew when to give me godly advice, when to set me straight, when to tan my hide, and when to hug my neck. You taught me love, respect, and manners, the building blocks for success in life. You kept it real and believed in me from the very beginning. I would like to express my deepest appreciation to you for setting me on the right path. I love and admire you both.

Allisyn Lambes: Do you know what I love about you? I never have to guess what's on your mind. What you see is what you get. And what I got in you is a wonderful sister who always has my back. I love you and thank you for being the person and sister you are.

Amy Goins: You are my sister from another mister, my BFF, the Thelma to my Louise, my ride or die. We are kindred spirits, you and I, and I'm honored to be traveling this path of life together.

To all my family: Brooks Varalla, Sean Lambes, Brantley Lambes, Mike Gravel, Janne Gravel, Mark Gravel, Krissy Gravel, Kinsey Gravel, Dylan Gravel, Owen Gravel, Hunter Davis: One of the biggest gifts I ever got was having you as my family. Not many people get to have such a cool squad.

Claudia Riemer Boutote, founder of Red Raven Studio: Where can I start? Without you, this book never would've happened. Thank you for your guidance, wisdom, elegance, and strength . . . and for shepherding this process from start to finish. I am deeply indebted to you, look up to you, and admire your grace!

Nancy French: You are the third Nancy to change my life forever. Your turn of phrase, way with words, and soulful depth is a God-given gift that I was blessed to experience. You get me. When I read your David Lee Roth article, I knew you were my partner for this book, and that we would be sisters for life!

Nelson Books / Thomas Nelson Team: It's been a surreal experience sitting down and writing a book—and it took a whole army. Thank you, **Andrew Stoddard**, vice president and publisher, for having a vision for this book. HUGE thank you to **Janet Talbert** for being an excellent executive editor on this project, and for making my writing even better. Your ideas, leadership, and heart for this message and the Lord is what connects us. Thank you to **Janene MacIvor** for serving as the production editor and all your behind-the-scenes work. Shout out to **Natalie Nyquist** too. **Claire Drake, Stephanie Tresner, Brian Scharp, Chris Sigfrids, Lisa Beech, Sarah van Cleve, LaTasha Estelle, Monica Jones,** and those whose names I may not know: Words cannot express my gratitude for your bold marketing and communications strategies which helped people find this book!

To everyone on the **sales team:** Thank you! I'm grateful.

Meg Schmidt, I love the cover, girl. **Phoebe Wetherbee,** you made the interior of the book look fantastic! **Aryana Hendrawan, and everyone in Production,** thank you for carrying this book over the finish line.

Huge gratitude to **Tracy Holland, Phil Berger, Earl Robinson, Kennedy Kero, Sanaz Memarian Huber, Ali Najafian,** and the **entire LWYA** family. Let's go!!!!!

Zac Miller, thank you for all your creative talent which helps me share my heart with the world every week in my podcast. Love you, my brother. Thank you, **Mike Kligerman** and **Kathleen Grant** for all your creative support on the podcast.

Jody Bell, Sara Noto, Sarah Thompson, Emily Bredin, Tara Ward, and the whole Belle Team: Thank you for bringing so much beauty into the world!

Susan Bramley, Jack Bramley, Leslie Dealba, Colleen Ginsburg, John Shrader, Kristy Destefano, Diane McKenna,

and the entire Thoughts Embellished team: Thank you for helping me create Belle by Kim Gravel®.

Thank you to **Heidi Krupp** and your entire public relations team for using your great skills to make a "difference"! Big props to **Jennifer Willingham, Jeff Roman,** and the entire **EPIC team**!

To my **QVC family** (and I do mean family): Thanks to the one and only **Jane Treacy** (Have you washed your Flexibelle's?), **Rachel Ungaro, Shannon Mallon,** and all the buyers, producers, and hosts who help make possible all things Belle. I love and appreciate you.

To everyone who has ever supported this message of confidence along the way: whether it was during the Beloved years, *Kim of Queens* television show, or the sisterhood of QVC. When I stand in front of the camera or microphone and speak, a miracle happens: you invite me into your home, your closet, your life . . . and we really connect.

We are the same, cut from the same cloth. We have the same insecurities. We share the same passions. We love our families and want the best for them and for ourselves.

We're friends.

Through the miracle of modern technology, we've somehow gotten to know each other in a way we never could've connected before, and I'm grateful. I want you to know I support you, because you are the backbone of our families, communities, and the world.

I appreciate that you—once again—are supporting me now by holding this book.

Thanks, y'all! Kim XX

Notes

Chapter 2: If You Ain't Dead, You Ain't Done!

1. Dan B. Allender, "Getting Caught by Your Calling," *Views from the Edge,* Mars Hill Graduate School, https://www.onelifemaps.com/wp-content/uploads/2015/04/Getting-Caught-By-Your-Calling.pdf, from Dan Allender, *To Be Told: God Invites You to Coauthor Your Future* (Colorado Springs: Waterbrook, 2005), 89–105.
2. Kittie L. Suffield, "Little Is Much When God Is in It," 1924. Public domain.
3. "History of Cologne Cathedral," Köln, https://www.cologne-tourism.com/see-experience/cologne-cathedral/history/.

Chapter 3: Don't Edit Your Story

1. Kimberly Paige Hardee, "For the First Time," *Collected Works,* (2006), https://open.spotify.com/track/4mvdqVnirMDuzwBoFQwnEt.
2. *Jerry Maguire,* directed by Cameron Crowe (Culver City, CA: Sony Pictures Releasing, 1996).
3. J. R. R. Tolkien, *The Fellowship of the Ring,* The Lord of the Rings, media tie-in edition (New York: Del Rey, 2022), 74.

Chapter 4: Never Put Yourself on Sale

1. Megan Leonhardt, "60% of Women Say They've Never Negotiated Their Salary—and Many Quit Their Job Instead," CNBC, January 31, 2020, https://www.cnbc.com/2020/01/31/women-more-likely-to-change-jobs-to-get-pay-increase.html.
2. Hannah Riley Bowles, "Why Women Don't Negotiate Their Job Offers," *Harvard Business Review,* June 19, 2014, https://hbr.org/2014/06/why-women-dont-negotiate-their-job-offers.
3. Dale Carnegie, *How to Win Friends and Influence People: The Only Book You Need to Lead You to Success* (1936; repr., New York: Gallery Books, 1998), 85.

Chapter 5: Life Is Like a Jelly Doughnut

1. *Chariots of Fire,* directed by Hugh Hudson, written by Colin Welland (Los Angeles: Twentieth Century Fox, 1981).

Chapter 7: The Mess Is the Message

1. *Pride and Prejudice,* directed by Joe Wright (Universal City, CA: Universal Pictures, 2005).
2. C. S. Lewis, *The Lion, the Witch, and the Wardrobe* (1950; repr., New York: HarperTrophy, 1994), 171.
3. Augustine, *Confessions,* Book XI, https://archive.org/stream/in.ernet.dli.2015.157225/2015.157225.The-Confessions-Of-St-Augustine_djvu.txt.

Chapter 9: Level Up, Buttercup!

1. *The Empire Strikes Back,* directed by Irvin Kershner, written by Lawrence Kasdan and Leight Brackett, story by George Lucas (San Francisco: Lucasfilm Ltd., 1980).

Chapter 10: Don't Let Anyone Call You Out of Your Name

1. W. C. Fields, quote widely attributed online.

Chapter 12: Fashioned for Greatness

1. Dan B. Allender, "Getting Caught by Your Calling," *Views from the Edge*, Mars Hill Graduate School, https://www.onelifemaps.com/wp-content/uploads/2015/04/Getting-Caught-By-Your-Calling.pdf, from Dan Allender, *To Be Told: God Invites You to Coauthor Your Future* (Colorado Springs: Waterbrook, 2005), 89–105.
2. Frederick Buechner, *A Room Called Remember: Uncollected Pieces* (San Francisco: HarperSanFrancisco, 1992), 5–6.
3. Buechner, *Room Called Remember*, 6.

About the Author

Credit: Sylvia Lee Photography

Kim Gravel is the host of a bevy of number-one shows on QVC and is a wildly successful entrepreneur, television personality, motivational speaker, life coach, host of *The Kim Gravel Show* podcast, and leader in the fashion and beauty industry. In 1991, Gravel was one of the youngest contestants to become Miss Georgia and later starred in Lifetime Network's hit docu-series *Kim of Queens.* In 2016 Kim launched her apparel line Belle by Kim Gravel® on QVC. In 2024 Gravel launched a new lifestyle brand Love Who You Are, which includes beauty, home, jewelry, and apparel. Kim lives outside Atlanta with her husband, Travis, and two sons.

◆ ◆ ◆

To take my confidence quiz and stay connected and up to date on all my confidence happenings, including live events, please scan the QR code with your phone's camera. Thanks! Xo, Kim

https://cc.kimgravel.com